CompTIA Security+:

Get Certified Get Ahead

SY0-301 Practice Test Questions

By Darril Gibson

Dedication

To my wife. Thanks for sharing your life with me and allowing me to share my life with you.

About the Author

Darril Gibson is an accomplished author and professional trainer. He has authored or coauthored more than a dozen books and contributed as a technical editor for many more books. He holds many current IT certifications including: CompTIA A+, Network+, Security+, (ISC)2 SSCP, CISSP, MCDST (XP), MCSA, MCSA Messaging (2000, 2003), MCSE (NT 4.0, 2000, 2003), MCDBA (SQL 7.0, 2000), MCITP (Vista, Server 2008, SQL 2005, SQL 2008), MCTS (Server 2008, SQL Server 2008), MCSD (6.0, .NET), and ITIL Foundations v 3.0.

He is the CEO of Security Consulting and Training, LLC and actively teaches, writes, and consults on a wide variety of IT topics including CompTIA Security+. He also teaches as an adjunct professor at ECPI University.

Darril lives in Virginia Beach with his wife and two dogs. Whenever possible, they escape to a small cabin in the country on over twenty acres of land that continues to provide peace, tranquility, and balance.

Acknowledgements

I'd like to express my thanks to the two technical editors on the CompTIA Security+: Get Certified Get Ahead SY0-301 Study Guide. Duane Gibson and Bill Talbott provided outstanding feedback on the study guide and the work they did on that book helped me get this book to print. Thanks again.

Table of Contents

Introduction

After completing the writing of the CompTIA Security+ Get Certified Get Ahead Study guide, I was a little dismayed at how long it was going to take to get to print. As a self-publisher, things just take a lot longer than they do with an established publishing company. However, I know there are many people that are studying for the SY0-301 Security+ exam and would value some practice test questions. I frequently

I pulled 280 questions out of the study guide and reformatted them for this practice test question guide, and that's what you have here. The Study Guide has a lot more content explaining all of the concepts and the content. However, if you're just looking for realistic practice test questions to test your knowledge, this book is for you.

It's organized into 6 chapters with each chapter covering one of the Security+ Domains. The chapters have different numbers of questions, based on the percent of examination content and the topics covered. The six Security+ domains are:

- **Network Security:** 21 percent of examination content
- **Compliance and Operational Security:** 18 percent of examination content
- **Threats and Vulnerabilities:** 21 percent of examination content
- **Application, Data and Host Security:** 16 percent of examination content

- **Access Control and Identity Management:** 13 percent of examination content

- **Cryptography:** 11 percent of examination content

CompTIA publishes a listing of the objectives on its web site. At this writing, this listing is accurate, but CompTIA includes the following disclaimers:

- *"The lists of examples provided in bulleted format below each objective are not exhaustive lists. Other examples of technologies, processes or tasks pertaining to each objective may also be included on the exam although not listed or covered in this objectives document."*

- *"The CompTIA Security+ Certification Exam Objectives are subject to change without notice."*

You can verify that the objectives haven't changed by checking on www.comptia.org.

As a side note, you can still take the SY0-201 exam until December 31, 2011. If you're pursuing that exam, The SY0-201 version of the CompTIA Security+: Get Certified Get Ahead: SY0-201 Study Guide is available on Amazon (ISBN-10: 1439236364.)

About the Exam

CompTIA first released the Security+ exam in 2002 and it has quickly grown in popularity. They revised the exam objectives 2008 and again in 2011. The 2011 exam is numbered as SY0-301 (or JK0-018 for the academic version of the exam). SY0-101 (the original version of CompTIA Security+) was retired in July 2009 and SY0-201 will retire on December 31, 2011.

A summary of the details of the exam includes:

- **Number of questions:** 100
- **Time to complete questions:** 90 minutes (does not include time to complete pre-test and post-test surveys)
- **Passing score:** 750
- **Grading criteria:** Scale of 100 to 900 (about 83 percent)
- **Question types:** Multiple choice
- **Exam format:** Traditional—can move back and forth to view previous questions
- **Exam prerequisites:** None required but Network+ is recommended
- **Exam test providers:** Prometric and Pearson Vue

Number of Questions and Duration

You have ninety minutes to complete one hundred questions. This gives you about one minute per question. Don't let this scare you; it's actually a good thing. With only about a minute to read and answer a question, you know the questions can't be very long.

Passing Score

A score of 750 is required to pass. This is on a scale of 100 to 900. If the exam is paid for, and you don't get a single question correct, you still get a score of 100. If you get every testable question correct, you get a score of 900.

If all questions are equal, then you need to get eighty-four questions correct—a passing score of 750 divided by 900 = .8333 or 83.33 percent. However, CompTIA doesn't say if all questions are scored equally or whether harder questions are weighted and worth more. A score of 83 percent is higher than many other certification exams so you shouldn't underestimate the difficulty of this exam. However, many people regularly pass it and you can pass it too. With this book, you will be well prepared.

Beta Questions

You exam may have some beta questions. They aren't graded but instead are used to test the validity of the questions. If everyone gets a beta question correct, it's probably too easy. If everyone gets it incorrect, there's probably something wrong with the question. After enough people have tested a beta question, it's analyzed and may be added to the test bank or rewritten and retested.

The good news is that CompTIA doesn't grade the beta questions. However, you don't know what questions are beta and what questions are valid, so you need to treat every question equally.

Question Types

Expect the questions on the exam to be straightforward. For example, what's 5 X 5? Either you know the answer is 25 or you don't. The exam questions test your knowledge of the material, not necessarily your ability to dissect the question so that you can figure out what the question is really trying to ask.

I'm not saying the knowledge is simplistic, only that the questions will be worded so that you can easily understand what they are asking.

As a comparative example, Microsoft certification questions can be quite complex. Microsoft questions often aren't just testing your knowledge of the topic but your ability to analyze the material and logically come to the right conclusion.

Here are two examples of questions—the first shows how Microsoft may word the question on a Microsoft certification exam, and the second shows how CompTIA may word it for the CompTIA Security+ exam.

- **Microsoft.** You are driving a bus from Chicago to Atlanta at 55 mph with twenty-two passengers. The bus is painted blue. At the same time, a train is traveling from Miami to Atlanta at 40 mph. The train has a yellow caboose. What color are the bus driver's eyes?

- **CompTIA Security+.** What color are your eyes?

Notice the first question adds a lot of superfluous information. Two pieces are critical to answering the first question. It starts by saying, "You are driving a bus..." and then ends by asking, "What color are the bus driver's eyes?" You're required to put the two together and weed through the irrelevant information to come to the correct answer.

The second question is straightforward. "What color are your eyes?" There's very little analysis required. Either you know it or you don't. This is what you can expect from most of the CompTIA Security+ questions.

Some of the CompTIA exam questions may have a little more detail than just a single sentence, but overall, expect them to be one- to two-sentence questions. They are only giving you about one minute for each question, and it's not intended to be a reading comprehension exam.

As an example, you may see a question like: "What port does HTTPS use?" In this case, you'd need to know that HTTPS uses port 443.

However, knowledge of expanded material could be tested by rewording it a little, such as: "What port needs to be opened to allow secure web server traffic?" In this case, you'd need to know that a web server uses HTTPS for secure web traffic, and HTTPS uses port 443.

You may also see questions that use phrases such as "best choice", "best description", or "most secure". In these examples, don't be surprised if you see two answers that could answer the question, while only one is the best choice. For example, which one of the following numbers is between 1 and 10 and is the highest: 1, 8, 14, 23. Clearly 1 and 8 are within 1 and 10, but 14 and 23 are not. However, only 8 is both within 1 and 10 and the highest.

Here is a more realistic, security related question that shows this:

Question: You have discovered a wireless base station using the same SSID as your wireless network. No one in your organization installed this. What best describes this?

    A. Rogue access point

    B. IV attack

    C. War driving

    D. Evil twin

This is a rogue access point since it isn't authorized. However, a *better* answer is that it is an evil twin (answer D.) since it's a rogue access point with the same SSID as your production environment. When you see key words like best, most, or highest, be careful not to jump on the first answer. There may be a more correct answer.

Exam Format

Questions are multiple-choice types where you choose one answer or multiple answers. When you need to choose multiple answers, the question may direct you to choose two, choose three, or choose all that apply.

You start at question 1 and go to question 100. During the process, you can mark any questions you want to review when you're done. Additionally, you can view previous questions if desired. For example, if you get to question 10 and then remember something that helps you answer question 5, you can go back and redo question 5.

Exam Prerequisites

All that is required for you to take the exam is money. Other than that, there are no enforced prerequisites.

However, to successfully pass the exam, you're expected to have at least two years of experience working with computers in a networking environment. If you have more than that, the exam materials will likely come easier to you. If you have less, the exam may be more difficult.

Exam Test Providers

You can take the exam at either a Pearson Vue or Prometric testing site. Some testing sites providing testing and nothing else. However, most testing sites are part of another company, such as a training company, college, or university. You can take an exam at the training company's testing site even if you haven't taken a course with them.

Both the Pearson Vue and the Prometric web sites include search tools you can use to find a testing site close to you. Check them out at http://www.vue.com and http://prometric.com.

At this writing, the CompTIA Security+ exam is $266 if you purchase it at full price. However, you can usually purchase discount vouchers for less than the retail price. If you want to pay less for the exam, use Google and enter "Security+ test voucher." You'll get several links to companies that sell vouchers at a discount.

When you purchase the voucher, you get the voucher number, and you can use this number to register at a testing site. A word of caution: make sure you purchase a voucher for the right testing center. If you purchase a Pearson Vue voucher, you won't be able to use it at a Prometric testing center unless they are also a Pearson Vue testing center. Some testing centers support both Vue and Prometric, but you should check first.

About the Study Guide

This book provides realiste practice test questions with answers. However, if you're looking for more than just practice test questions for the CompTIA Security+ SY0-301 exam, check out the CompTIA Security+: Get Certified Get Ahead: SY0-301 Study Guide. That book is an update to my SY0-201 guide, which helped thousands of readers pass the exam the first time they took it.

The study guide covers every aspect of the SY0-301 exam, and includes the same elements readers raved about in the previous version. Each of the eleven chapters presents topics in an easy to understand manner and includes real-world examples of security principles in action. I used many of the same analogies and explanations I honed in the classroom that have helped hundreds of students master the Security+ content. You'll understand the important and relevant security topics for the Security+ exam, without being overloaded with unnecessary details. Additionally, each chapter includes a comprehensive review section to help you focus on what's important.

With over 450 realistic practice test questions with in-depth explanations, the book also includes a 100 question pre-test, a 100 question post-test, and practice test questions at the end of every chapter to help you test your comprehension and readiness for the exam. Each practice test question includes a detailed explanation to help you understand the content and the reasoning behind the question. You'll be ready to take and pass the exam the first time you take it.

If you plan to pursue any of the advanced security certifications, the study guide will also help you lay a solid foundation of security knowledge. Learn the material, and you'll be a step ahead for other exams. The CompTIA Security+: Get Certified Get Ahead: SY0-301 Study Guide is for any IT or security professional interested in advancing in their field, and a must read for anyone striving to master the basics of IT systems security.

The book isn't available at this writing, but it will be soon. Check out Amazon using one of the following ISBNs, or search Amazon using "Darril Gibson".

ISBN-13: 978-1463762360

ISBN-10: 1463762364

For more information on this and other resources related to Security+, check out http://sec-plus.com

Chapter 1 Network Security

Network Security topics are **21 percent** of the CompTIA Security+ exam. The objectives in this domain are:

1.1 Explain the security function and purpose of network devices and technologies

- Firewalls
- Routers
- Switches
- Load Balancers
- Proxies
- Web security gateways
- VPN concentrators
- NIDS and NIPS (Behavior based, signature based, anomaly based, heuristic)
- Protocol analyzers
- Sniffers
- Spam filter, all-in-one security appliances
- Web application firewall vs. network firewall
- URL filtering, content inspection, malware inspection

1.2 Apply and implement secure network administration principles
- Rule-based management
- Firewall rules
- VLAN management
- Secure router configuration
- Access control lists
- Port Security
- 802.1x
- Flood guards
- Loop protection
- Implicit deny

- Prevent network bridging by network separation
- Log analysis

1.3 Distinguish and differentiate network design elements and compounds
- DMZ
- Subnetting
- VLAN
- NAT
- Remote Access
- Telephony
- NAC
- Virtualization
- Cloud Computing
  o Platform as a Service
  o Software as a Service
  o Infrastructure as a Service

1.4 Implement and use common protocols
- IPSec
- SNMP
- SSH
- DNS
- TLS
- SSL
- TCP/IP
- FTPS
- HTTPS
- SFTP
- SCP
- ICMP
- IPv4 vs. IPv6

1.5 Identify commonly used default network ports
- FTP
- SFTP
- FTPS
- TFTP
- TELNET
- HTTP
- HTTPS
- SCP
- SSH
- NetBIOS

1.6 Implement wireless network in a secure manner
- WPA
- WPA2
- WEP
- EAP
- PEAP
- LEAP
- MAC filter
- SSID broadcast
- TKIP
- CCMP
- Antenna Placement
- Power level controls

The CompTIA Security+: Get Certified Get Ahead SY0-301 Study Guide (ISBN 1463762364) discusses these topics in much more depth. Sec-plus.com has more details on the availability of this book.

√ **Get Certified**
  √ **Get Ahead**

Practice Test Questions
for Network Security Domain

1. Your organization uses switches for connectivity. Of the following choices, what will protect the switch?

    A. Disable unused MAC addresses

    B. Disable unused ports

    C. Disable unused IPv4 addresses

    D. Disable unused IPv6 addresses

2. Of the following choices, what represents the best choice to prevent intrusions on an individual computer?

    A. HIDS

    B. NIDS

    C. Host-based firewall

    D. Network-based firewalls

3. Of the following choices, what controls traffic between networks?

    A. A firewall

    B. Load balancer

    C. VPN concentrator

    D. Protocol analyzer

4. An organization has a web security gateway installed. What function is this performing?

    A. MAC filtering

B. Caching content

C. Hiding internal IP addresses

D. Content filtering

5. Your organization hosts a large web site served by multiple servers. They need to optimize the workload and distribute it equally among all the servers. What should they use?

A. Proxy server

B. Load balancer

C. Web security gateway

D. Security appliance

6. Of the following choices, what is the best choice for a device to filter and cache content from web pages?

A. Web security gateway

B. VPN concentrator

C. Proxy server

D. MAC filtering

7. What can an administrator use to detect malicious activity after it occurred?

A. Firewall

B. Sniffer

C. Port scanner

D. IDS

8. Of the following choices, what would detect compromises on a local server?

    A. HIDS

    B. NIPS

    C. Firewall

    D. Protocol analyzer

9. Of the following choices, what represents the best choice for a system to detect attacks on a network, but not block them?

    A. NIDS

    B. NIPS

    C. HIDS

    D. HIPS

10. Your organization is using a NIDS. The NIDS vendor regularly provides updates for the NIDS to detect known attacks. What type of NIDS is this?

    A. Anomaly-based

    B. Signature-based

    C. Prevention-based

    D. Honey-based

11. You are preparing to deploy an anomaly-based detection system to monitor network activity. What would you create first?

    A. Flood guards

    B. Signatures

    C. Baseline

D. Honeypot

12. Of the following choices, what best describes the function of an IPS?

    A. Detect attacks

    B. Stop attacks in progress

    C. Prevent attackers from attacking

    D. Notify appropriate personnel of attacks

13. Of the following choices, what provides active protection for an operating system?

    A. NIDS

    B. NIPS

    C. HIDS

    D. HIPS

14. Of the following choices, what most accurately describes a NIPS?

    A. Detects and takes action against threats

    B. Provides notification of threats

    C. Detects and eliminates threats

    D. Identifies zero day vulnerabilities

15. An IPS is monitoring data streams looking for malicious behavior. When it detects malicious behavior, it blocks the traffic. What is this IPS using?

    A. Smurf detection

    B. Honeypot

C. Content inspection

D. Port scanner

16. A user plugged a cable into two RJ-45 wall jacks connected to unused ports on a switch. In a short period, this disrupted the overall network performance. What should you do to protect against this problem in the future?

A. Enable loop protection on the switch

B. Disable port security

C. Use a VLAN

D. Create DMZ

17. What can you use to logically separate computers in two different departments within a company?

A. A hub

B. A VLAN

C. NAT

D. A flood guard

18. Most firewalls have a default rule placed at the end of the firewall's ACL. Which of the following is the most likely default rule?

A. Deny any any

B. Deny ICMP all

C. Allow all all

D. Allow TCP all

19. Of the following choices, what best describes a method of managing the flow of network traffic by allowing or denying traffic based on ports, protocols, and addresses?

    A. Implicit deny

    B. Firewall rules

    C. Proxy server content filter

    D. Firewall logs

20. Your network includes a subnet that hosts accounting servers with sensitive data. You want to ensure that users in the Marketing department (on a separate subnet) cannot access these servers. Of the following choices, what would be the easiest to achieve the goal?

    A. Enable load balancing

    B. Enable port security

    C. Use an ACL

    D. Add a host-based firewall to each server.

21. You are deploying a remote access server for your organization. Employees will use this to access the network while on the road. Of the following choices, what must you configure?

    A. NAC

    B. ACLs

    C. MACs

    D. NAT-T

22 You are reviewing a firewall's ACL and see the following statement: **drop all**. What security principle does this enforce?

    A. Least privilege

    B. Integrity

    C. Availability

    D. Implicit deny

23. Firewalls include rules in an ACL. Which of the following would block network traffic that isn't in any of the previously defined rules?

    A. Explicit allow

    B. Implicit allow

    C. Explicit deny

    D. Implicit deny

24. An organization recently created a security policy. Of the following choices, what is a technical implementation of security policy?

    A. Training

    B. Acceptable use acknowledgement

    C. Implicit deny rule in a firewall

    D. Job rotation

25. Which of the following IP addresses are on the same subnet? (Choose all that apply.)

    A. 192.168.1.50, 255.255.255.192

    B. 192.168.1.100, 255.255.255.192

    C. 192.168.1.165, 255.255.255.192

    D. 192.168.1.189, 255.255.255.192

26. Of the following choices, what can be used to allow access to specific services from the Internet while protecting access to an internal network?

    A. SSH

    B. Implicit deny

    C. DMZ

    D. Port security

27. Of the following choices, what hides the IP addresses of computers inside a network from computers outside the network?

    A. Web security gateway

    B. Replacing all hubs with switches

    C. WAF

    D. NAT

28. Your organization is creating a site-to-site VPN tunnel between the main business location and a remote office. What can they use to create the tunnel?

    A. WPA2-Enterprise

    B. RADIUS

    C. NAC

    D. IPsec

29. You are planning to deploy a VPN with IPsec. Users will use the VPN to access corporate resources while they are on the road. How should you use IPsec?

    A. With AH in tunnel mode

B. With AH in transport mode

C. With ESP in tunnel mode

D. With ESP in transport mode

30. An employee connects to the corporate network using a VPN. However, the client is not able to access internal resources, but instead receives a warning indicating their system is not up-to-date with current patches. What is causing this behavior?

A. The VPN is using IPsec

B. The VPN is not using IPsec

C. NAC is disabled on the network and remediation must take place before the client can access internal resources

D. NAC is enabled on the network and remediation must take place before the client can access internal resources

31. What technology can an organization use to assist with computing requirements in heavily utilized systems?

A. ISP

B. DLP

C. Cloud computing

D. Remote wipe

32. Employees in your organization access web-based email using cloud-based technologies. What type of technology is this?

A. IaaS

B. PaaS

C. SaaS

D. Network-based DLP

33. Of the following choices, what is the best explanation of what a PaaS provides to customers?

    A. Web-based applications provided over the Internet.

    B. A device that reduces the risk of employees emailing confidential information outside the organization

    C. Protection against VM escape attacks

    D. An easy-to-configure operating system and on-demand computing capabilities

34. An organization is considering using virtualization in their datacenter. What benefits will this provide? (Choose all that apply.)

    A. Increased footprint

    B. Decreased footprint

    C. Reduction in physical equipment needing security

    D. Elimination of VM escape attacks

35. An organization wants to hide addresses it uses on its internal network. What can assist with this goal?

    A. MAC filtering

    B. NAC

    C. NAT

    D. DMZ

36. What type of attack starts on a virtual system but can affect the physical host?

    A. TPM

    B. DLP

    C. VM escape

    D. VMware

37. Which of the following protocols is a file transfer protocol using SSH?

    A. SFTP

    B. TFTP

    C. SICMP

    D. CCMP

38. Of the following choices, which one provides the most security for FTP?

    A. FTP active mode

    B. FTPS

    C. TFTP

    D. SCP

39. Of the following choices, what is a benefit of IPsec?

    A. MAC filtering

    B. Flood guard

    C. Load balancing

    D. Payload encryption

40. What protocol is used to monitor and configure network devices?

    A. ICMP

    B. SFTP

    C. SNMP

    D. DNS

41. Which of the following is an IPv6 address?

    A. 192.168.1.100

    B. 192.168.1.100 /128

    C. FE80:20D4:3FF7:003F:DE62

    D. FE80:0000:0000:0000:20D4:3FF7:003F:DE62

42. An administrator decides to block Telnet access to an internal network from any remote device on the Internet. Which of the following is the best choice to accomplish this?

    A. Block port 22 at the host firewall

    B. Block port 22 on internal routers

    C. Block port 23 at the network firewall

    D. Block port 23 on internal routers

43. What port does SFTP use?

    A. 22

    B. 23

    C. 443

    D. 1443

44. What ports do HTTP and HTTPS use?

    A. 20 and 21

    B. 22 and 25

    C. 80 and 443

    D. 80 and 1433

45. What port does SMTP use?

    A. 22

    B. 25

    C. 110

    D. 143

46. Of the following choices, what ports are used by NetBIOS? (Choose two.)

    A. 80

    B. 137

    C. 139

    D. 3389

47. You've recently completed a wireless audit and realize that the wireless signal from your company's WAP reaches the parking lot. What can you do to ensure that the signal doesn't reach outside your building?

    A. Increase the WAP's power level

    B. Decrease the WAP's power level

    C. Enable SSID broadcasting

    D. Disable SSID broadcasting

48. Your organization is designing an 802.11n network and they want to use the strongest security. What would you recommend?

    A. FTPS

    B. SSL

    C. WEP

    D. WPA2

49. Which of the following authentication mechanisms can provide centralized authentication for a wireless network?

    A. WPA2

    B. RADIUS

    C. Multifactor authentication

    D. Kerberos

50. You want to ensure that only specific wireless clients can access your wireless networks. Of the following choices, what provides the best solution?

    A. MAC filtering

    B. Content filtering

    C. NAT

    D. NIPS

51. You recently completed a wireless audit of your company's wireless network. You've identified several unknown devices connected to the network and realize they are devices owned by company employees. What can you use to prevent these devices from connecting?

    A. MAC filtering

B. Enable SSID broadcast

C. Enable isolation mode on the WAP

D. Reduce the power levels on the WAP

52. What can you do to prevent the easy discovery of a WAP?

A. Enable MAC filtering

B. Disable SSID broadcast

C. Enable SSID broadcast

D. Enable 802.1X authentication

Practice Test Questions with Answers
for Network Security Domain

1. Your organization uses switches for connectivity. Of the following choices, what will protect the switch?

    A. Disable unused MAC addresses

    B. Disable unused ports

    C. Disable unused IPv4 addresses

    D. Disable unused IPv6 addresses

1. **B** is correct. Disabling unused ports is a part of basic port security.

A is incorrect. While switches can associate MAC addresses associated with ports, it's not possible to disable unused MAC addresses on the switch.

C and D are incorrect. Switches track traffic based on MAC addresses, not IP addresses.

Objective: 1.1 Explain the security function and purpose of network devices and technologies

2. Of the following choices, what represents the best choice to prevent intrusions on an individual computer?

    A. HIDS

    B. NIDS

    C. Host-based firewall

    D. Network-based firewalls

2. **C** is correct. A host-based firewall can help prevent intrusions on individual computers such as a server or desktop computer.

A and B are incorrect. A host-based intrusion detection system (HIDS) and a network-based intrusion detection system (NIDS) can *detect* intrusions, not *prevent* them.

D is incorrect. A network-based firewall is used to monitor and control traffic on a network, not just an individual system.

Objective: 1.1 Explain the security function and purpose of network devices and technologies

3. Of the following choices, what controls traffic between networks?

    A. A firewall

    B. Load balancer

    C. VPN concentrator

    D. Protocol analyzer

3. **A** is correct. A firewall controls traffic between networks using rules within an ACL.

B is incorrect. A load balancer can optimize and distribute data loads across multiple computers.

C is incorrect. A VPN concentrator provides access to an internal network from a public network such as the Internet.

D is incorrect. A protocol analyzer (a sniffer) is used to view headers and clear-text contents in IP packets, but it can't control the traffic.

Objective: 1.1 Explain the security function and purpose of network devices and technologies

4. An organization has a web security gateway installed. What function is this performing?

    A. MAC filtering

    B. Caching content

    C. Hiding internal IP addresses

    D. Content filtering

4. **D** is correct. A web security gateway performs content filtering (including filtering for malicious attachments, malicious code, blocked URLs and more).

A is incorrect. Port security and network access control use MAC filtering to limit access.

B is incorrect. A proxy server caches content.

C is incorrect. NAT translates public IP addresses to private IP addresses, private back to public, and can hide addresses on the internal network.

Objective: 1.1 Explain the security function and purpose of network devices and technologies

5. Your organization hosts a large web site served by multiple servers. They need to optimize the workload and distribute it equally among all the servers. What should they use?

    A. Proxy server

    B. Load balancer

    C. Web security gateway

    D. Security appliance

5. **B** is correct. A load balancer can optimize and distribute data loads across multiple computers or multiple networks.

A is incorrect. A proxy server provides content filtering and caching.

C and D are incorrect. Web security gateways and all-in-one security appliances provide content filtering, but not load balancing.

Objective: 1.1 Explain the security function and purpose of network devices and technologies

6. Of the following choices, what is the best choice for a device to filter and cache content from web pages?

    A. Web security gateway

    B. VPN concentrator

    C. Proxy server

    D. MAC filtering

6. **C** is correct. A proxy server includes the ability to filter and cache content from web pages.

A is incorrect. A web security gateway can filter web-based content, but it doesn't always have caching capabilities.

B is incorrect. A VPN concentrator provides access to VPN clients.

D is incorrect. MAC filtering can be used with port security on a switch, but doesn't filter web page content.

Objective: 1.1 Explain the security function and purpose of network devices and technologies

7. What can an administrator use to detect malicious activity after it occurred?

    A. Firewall

    B. Sniffer

    C. Port scanner

    D. IDS

7. **D** is correct. An intrusion detection system (IDS) detects malicious activity after it has occurred.

A is incorrect. A firewall attempts to prevent attacks.

B is incorrect. A sniffer can capture and analyze packets to read data or inspect IP headers.

C is incorrect. A port scanner looks for open ports on a system to determine running services and protocols.

Objective: 1.1 Explain the security function and purpose of network devices and technologies

8. Of the following choices, what would detect compromises on a local server?

    A. HIDS

    B. NIPS

    C. Firewall

    D. Protocol analyzer

8. **A** is correct. A host-based intrusion detection system (HIDS) can detect attacks (including successful attacks resulting in compromises) on local systems such as workstations and servers.

B is incorrect. A NIPS detects and mitigates attacks on a network, not local systems.

C is incorrect. A firewall attempts to prevent attacks not detect them.

D is incorrect. A protocol analyzer can capture and analyze packets, but it will not detect attacks.

Objective: 1.1 Explain the security function and purpose of network devices and technologies

9. Of the following choices, what represents the best choice for a system to detect attacks on a network, but not block them?

> A. NIDS
>
> B. NIPS
>
> C. HIDS
>
> D. HIPS

9. **A** is correct. A network-based intrusion detection system (NIDS) will detect attacks, but will not necessarily block them (unless it is an active NIDS).

B is incorrect. In contrast, a network-based intrusion prevention system will detect and block attacks.

C and D are incorrect. Host-based systems (HIDS and HIPS) provide protection for hosts, not networks.

Objective: 1.1 Explain the security function and purpose of network devices and technologies

10. Your organization is using a NIDS. The NIDS vendor regularly provides updates for the NIDS to detect known attacks. What type of NIDS is this?

    A. Anomaly-based

    B. Signature-based

    C. Prevention-based

    D. Honey-based

10. **B** is correct. Signature-based, network-based intrusion detection systems (NIDS) use signatures similar to antivirus software, which are downloaded regularly as updates.

A is incorrect. An anomaly-based (also called heuristic or behavior-based) detection system compares current activity with a previously created baseline to detect any anomalies or changes.

C is incorrect. An IPS is prevention based, but an IDS is detection based.

D is incorrect. There is no such thing as honey-based.

Objective: 1.1 Explain the security function and purpose of network devices and technologies

11. You are preparing to deploy an anomaly-based detection system to monitor network activity. What would you create first?

    A. Flood guards

    B. Signatures

    C. Baseline

    D. Honeypot

11. **C** is correct. An anomaly-based (also called heuristic or behavior-based) detection system compares current activity with a previously created baseline to detect any anomalies or changes.

A is incorrect. Flood guards help protect against SYN flood attacks.

B is incorrect. Signature-based systems use signatures similar to antivirus software.

D is incorrect. A honeypot is a server designed to look valuable to an attacker and can divert attacks.

Objective: 1.1 Explain the security function and purpose of network devices and technologies

12. Of the following choices, what best describes the function of an IPS?

    A. Detect attacks

    B. Stop attacks in progress

    C. Prevent attackers from attacking

    D. Notify appropriate personnel of attacks

12. **B** is correct. The primary purpose of an intrusion prevention system (IPS) is to stop attacks in progress.

A is incorrect. While an IPS detects attacks just as an IDS does, a distinguishing factor between an IDS and an IPS is that an IPS can also stop attacks in progress.

C is incorrect. It's not possible to prevent attackers from attacking, but an IPS can reduce the impact they have on a system.

D is incorrect. Both IDSs and IPSs will provide notifications.

Objective: 1.1 Explain the security function and purpose of network devices and technologies

13. Of the following choices, what provides active protection for an operating system?

    A. NIDS

    B. NIPS

    C. HIDS

    D. HIPS

13. **D is** correct. A host-based intrusion prevention system (HIPS) provides active protection for an individual host, including its operating system.

A and B are incorrect. Network based IDSs and IPSs monitor and protect network traffic.

C is incorrect. HIDS is passive by default.

Objective: 1.1 Explain the security function and purpose of network devices and technologies

14. Of the following choices, what most accurately describes a NIPS?

    A. Detects and takes action against threats

    B. Provides notification of threats

    C. Detects and eliminates threats

    D. Identifies zero day vulnerabilities

14. **A** is correct. A network-based intrusion prevention system (NIPS) attempts to detect and mitigate threats by taking action to block them.

B is incorrect. While a NIPS does provide notification, a distinguishing difference from a NIDS and a NIPS is that a NIPS takes action to stop the attack.

C is incorrect. Threats can't be eliminated.

D is incorrect. An anomaly-based IDS or IPS may be able to identify zero day vulnerabilities, though honeypots are used more often to detect zero day vulnerabilities.

Objective: 1.1 Explain the security function and purpose of network devices and technologies

15. An IPS is monitoring data streams looking for malicious behavior. When it detects malicious behavior, it blocks the traffic. What is this IPS using?

    A. Smurf detection

    B. Honeypot

    C. Content inspection

    D. Port scanner

15. **C** is correct. Many intrusion prevention systems (IPSs) use content inspection techniques to monitor data streams in search of malicious code or behaviors.

A is incorrect. Smurf is a type of attack, not a method of detection.

B is incorrect. A honeypot is a server designed to look valuable to an attacker, can divert attacks, and help organizations identify the latest unknown attacks.

D is incorrect. A port scanner looks for open ports on a system to determine running services and protocols.

Objective: 1.1 Explain the security function and purpose of network devices and technologies

16. A user plugged a cable into two RJ-45 wall jacks connected to unused ports on a switch. In a short period, this disrupted the overall network performance. What should you do to protect against this problem in the future?

    A. Enable loop protection on the switch

    B. Disable port security

    C. Use a VLAN

    D. Create DMZ

16. **A** is correct. Loop protection such as Spanning Tree Protocol (STP) protects against the switching loop problem described in the scenario.

B is incorrect. While disabling unused ports may help against this problem, you do this by implementing port security, not disabling port security.

C is incorrect. A DMZ is used to host Internet facing servers and isn't relevant in this situation.

D is incorrect. VLANs can logically separate computers using the same switch but do not prevent switching loops.

Objective: 1.2 Apply and implement secure network administration principles

17. What can you use to logically separate computers in two different departments within a company?

    A. A hub

    B. A VLAN

    C. NAT

    D. A flood guard

17. **B** is correct. A virtual local area network (VLAN) can group several different computers into a virtual network, or logically separate the computers in two different departments.

A is incorrect. A hub doesn't have any intelligence and can't separate the computers.

C is incorrect. NAT translates private IP addresses to public IP addresses, and public back to private.

D is incorrect. A flood guard protects against SYN flood attacks.

Objective: 1.2 Apply and implement secure network administration principles

18. Most firewalls have a default rule placed at the end of the firewall's ACL. Which of the following is the most likely default rule?

    A. Deny any any

    B. Deny ICMP all

    C. Allow all all

    D. Allow TCP all

18. **A** is correct. A **deny any any** or **drop all** statement is placed at the end of an ACL and enforces an implement deny strategy.

B is incorrect. While many firewalls include a rule to deny ICMP traffic (such as pings or ICMP sweeps), it isn't a default rule and wouldn't be placed last.

C is incorrect. An **allow all all** rule allows all protocol traffic that wasn't previously blocked but is rarely (if ever) used in a firewall.

D is incorrect. It's rare to allow all TCP traffic on any port. Instead, a firewall uses an implicit deny principle by specifying what is allowed, and blocking everything else.

Objective: 1.2 Apply and implement secure network administration principles

19. Of the following choices, what best describes a method of managing the flow of network traffic by allowing or denying traffic based on ports, protocols, and addresses?

    A. Implicit deny

    B. Firewall rules

    C. Proxy server content filter

    D. Firewall logs

19. **B** is correct. Firewalls use firewall rules (or rules within an ACL) to identify what traffic is allowed and what traffic is denied. A basic packet filtering firewall can filter traffic based on ports, protocols, and addresses.

A is incorrect. Firewalls use implicit deny to block all traffic not previously allowed, but this more accurately describes what is blocked rather describing the entire flow of traffic.

C is incorrect. A proxy server content filter can filter traffic based on content (such as URLs), but can't allow or deny traffic based on ports or protocols.

D is incorrect. Firewall logs are useful to determine what traffic a firewall has allowed or blocked but do not allow or deny traffic themselves.

Objective: 1.2 Apply and implement secure network administration principles

20. Your network includes a subnet that hosts accounting servers with sensitive data. You want to ensure that users in the Marketing department (on a separate subnet) cannot access these servers. Of the following choices, what would be the easiest to achieve the goal?

    A. Enable load balancing

    B. Enable port security

    C. Use an ACL

    D. Add a host-based firewall to each server.

20. **C** is correct. An access control list (ACL) on a router can block access to the subnet from another subnet.

A is incorrect. A load balancer can optimize and distribute data loads across multiple computers or multiple networks, but it doesn't isolate traffic.

B is incorrect. Disabling unused ports is a part of basic port security, and wouldn't separate subnet traffic.

D is incorrect. A host-based firewall can protect against intrusions on individual systems and could block the traffic but you'd have to enable it on every server, as opposed to creating a single rule in an ACL.

Objective: 1.2 Apply and implement secure network administration principles

21. You are deploying a remote access server for your organization. Employees will use this to access the network while on the road. Of the following choices, what must you configure?

    A. NAC

    B. ACLs

    C. MACs

    D. NAT-T

21. **B** is correct. Access control lists within a firewall must include rules to open the appropriate ports.

A and C are incorrect. NAC increases security and can filter traffic based on MAC addresses, but neither is required for remote access.

D is incorrect. NAT-T can circumvent problems related to IPsec usage, but it is not requirement for all remote access.

Objective: 1.2 Apply and implement secure network administration principles

22 You are reviewing a firewall's ACL and see the following statement: **drop all**. What security principle does this enforce?

    A. Least privilege

    B. Integrity

C. Availability

D. Implicit deny

22. **D** is correct. A **drop all** or **deny any any** statement is placed at the end of an access control list (ACL) and enforces an implement deny strategy.

A is incorrect. Least privilege ensures users only have the access they need to perform their jobs and no more.

B and C are incorrect. Integrity provides assurances that data has not been modified, and availability ensures systems and data are up and operational when needed, but the **drop all** statement doesn't address either of these as directly as implicit deny.

C is incorrect.

Objective: 1.2 Apply and implement secure network administration principles

23. Firewalls include rules in an ACL. Which of the following would block network traffic that isn't in any of the previously defined rules?

    A. Explicit allow

    B. Implicit allow

    C. Explicit deny

    D. Implicit deny

23. **D** is correct. Most firewalls have an implicit deny statement (such as **drop all** or **deny any any**) at the end of an access control list (ACL) to block all traffic not previously allowed.

A and B are incorrect. An allow rule would not block traffic.

C is incorrect. An explicit deny rule explicitly blocks traffic defined in the rule only, not all other traffic.

Objective: 1.2 Apply and implement secure network administration principles

24. An organization recently created a security policy. Of the following choices, what is a technical implementation of security policy?

    A. Training

    B. Acceptable use acknowledgement

    C. Implicit deny rule in a firewall

    D. Job rotation

24. **C** is correct. Firewall rules (including the implicit deny rule) provide technical implementation of security policies. The other choices are not technical controls.

A is incorrect. Organizations provide security awareness training to reinforce user compliance with security policies and to minimize the risk posed by users.

B is incorrect. It's common to have users sign an acceptable use statement when hired and periodically afterwards such as during annual security refresher training.

D is incorrect. Job rotation policies require employees to change roles on a regular basis.

Objective: 1.2 Apply and implement secure network administration principles

25. Which of the following IP addresses are on the same subnet? (Choose all that apply.)

    A. 192.168.1.50, 255.255.255.192

    B. 192.168.1.100, 255.255.255.192

    C. 192.168.1.165, 255.255.255.192

    D. 192.168.1.189, 255.255.255.192

25. **C** and **D** are correct. Both 192.168.1.165 and 192.168.1.189 are on the same subnet since bits 25 and 26 are the same (10). If a calculator is needed on the exam (such as for a problem like this), it will be available.

A and B are incorrect. Bits 25 and 26 are 00 for 192.168.1.50, and 01 for 192.168.1.100 so these two are on different subnets from the any of the other IP addresses.

Objective: 1.3 Distinguish and differentiate network design elements and compounds

26. Of the following choices, what can be used to allow access to specific services from the Internet while protecting access to an internal network?

    A. SSH

    B. Implicit deny

    C. DMZ

    D. Port security

26. **C** is correct. A demilitarized zone (DMZ) can provide access to services (hosted on servers) from the Internet while providing a layer of protection for the internal network.

A is incorrect. SSH encrypts traffic such as Telnet, SCP, and SFTP over port 22, but it can't control access.

B is incorrect. Implicit deny blocks all traffic not explicitly allowed.

D is incorrect. Port security enhances switch security and includes disabling unused ports.

Objective: 1.3 Distinguish and differentiate network design elements and compounds

27. Of the following choices, what hides the IP addresses of computers inside a network from computers outside the network?

    A. Web security gateway

    B. Replacing all hubs with switches

    C. WAF

    D. NAT

27. **D** is correct. Network Address Translation (NAT) translates public IP addresses to private IP addresses, and private back to public and hides addresses on the internal network.

A is incorrect. A Web security gateway performs content filtering, including filtering for malicious attachments, malicious code, blocked URLs and more.

B is incorrect. Replacing hubs with switches improves network performance and adds security, but doesn't hide addresses outside of a network.

C is incorrect. A web application firewall (WAF) is an additional firewall designed to protect a web application.

Objective: 1.3 Distinguish and differentiate network design elements and compounds

28. Your organization is creating a site-to-site VPN tunnel between the main business location and a remote office. What can they use to create the tunnel?

> A. WPA2-Enterprise
>
> B. RADIUS
>
> C. NAC
>
> D. IPsec

28. **D** is correct. IPsec is one of many tunneling protocols the organization can use to create a VPN tunnel.

A is incorrect. WPA2-Enterprise is a secure wireless protocol that includes authentication using an 802.1X server (often implemented as RADIUS).

B is incorrect. RADIUS provides authentication but doesn't create a tunnel.

C is incorrect. NAC provides security for clients such as inspecting them for health, but doesn't create the tunnel.

Objective: 1.3 Distinguish and differentiate network design elements and compounds, 1.4 Implement and use common protocols

29. You are planning to deploy a VPN with IPsec. Users will use the VPN to access corporate resources while they are on the road. How should you use IPsec?

    A. With AH in tunnel mode

    B. With AH in transport mode

    C. With ESP in tunnel mode

    D. With ESP in transport mode

29. **C** is correct. Encapsulating Security Payload (ESP) in tunnel mode encapsulates the entire IP packets and provides confidentiality, integrity, and authentication.

A is incorrect. AH only provides integrity and authentication.

B and D are incorrect. Transport mode doesn't encrypt the entire IP packets, and is used internally within a private network, not with a VPN.

Objective: 1.3 Distinguish and differentiate network design elements and compounds, 1.4 Implement and use common protocols

30. An employee connects to the corporate network using a VPN. However, the client is not able to access internal resources, but instead receives a warning indicating their system is not up-to-date with current patches. What is causing this behavior?

    A. The VPN is using IPsec

    B. The VPN is not using IPsec

    C. NAC is disabled on the network and remediation must take place before the client can access internal resources

D. NAC is enabled on the network and remediation must take place before the client can access internal resources

30. **D** is correct. Network access control (NAC) inspects clients for specific health conditions and can redirect access to a remediation network for unhealthy clients.

A and B are incorrect. NAC is not dependent on the tunneling protocol (such as IPsec).

C is incorrect. The warning would not appear if NAC was disabled.

Objective: 1.3 Distinguish and differentiate network design elements and compounds

31. What technology can an organization use to assist with computing requirements in heavily utilized systems?

    A. ISP

    B. DLP

    C. Cloud computing

    D. Remote wipe

31. **C** is correct. Cloud computing is very useful for heavily utilized systems and networks, and cloud providers provide the services.

A is incorrect. An ISP provides access to the Internet.

B is incorrect. A network-based DLP can examine and analyze network traffic and detect if confidential company data is included.

D is incorrect. Remote wipe can erase data on lost mobile devices such as mobile phones.

Objective: 1.3 Distinguish and differentiate network design elements and compounds

32. Employees in your organization access web-based email using cloud-based technologies. What type of technology is this?

    A. IaaS

    B. PaaS

    C. SaaS

    D. Network-based DLP

32. **C** is correct. Applications such as web-based email provided over the Internet are Software as a Service (SaaS) cloud-based technologies.
A is incorrect. Organizations use IaaS to rent access to hardware such as servers to limit their hardware footprint and personnel costs.
B is incorrect. PaaS provides cloud customers with an easy-to-configure operating system, and on-demand computing capabilities.
D is incorrect. A DLP is a device that reduces the risk of employees emailing confidential information outside the organization.
Objective: 1.3 Distinguish and differentiate network design elements and compounds

33. Of the following choices, what is the best explanation of what a PaaS provides to customers?

    A. Web-based applications provided over the Internet.

    B. A device that reduces the risk of employees emailing confidential information outside the organization

    C. Protection against VM escape attacks

D. An easy-to-configure operating system and on-demand computing capabilities

33. **D** is correct. Platform as a Service (PaaS) provides cloud customers with an easy-to-configure operating system and on-demand computing capabilities.

A is incorrect. Applications such as web-based email provided over the Internet are Software as a Service (SaaS) cloud-based technologies.

B is incorrect. A network-based DLP is a device that reduces the risk of employees emailing confidential information outside the organization.

C is incorrect. Keeping systems up-to-date protects virtual systems from VM escape attacks but PaaS does not provide this protection.

Objective: 1.3 Distinguish and differentiate network design elements and compounds

34. An organization is considering using virtualization in their datacenter. What benefits will this provide? (Choose all that apply.)

    A. Increased footprint

    B. Decreased footprint

    C. Reduction in physical equipment needing security

    D. Elimination of VM escape attacks

34. **B** and **C** are correct. Virtualization can reduce the footprint of a datacenter, eliminate wasted resources, and result in less physical equipment needing physical security.

A is incorrect. Virtualization reduces the footprint, not increases it.

D is incorrect. Virtual systems are susceptible to VM escape attacks if they aren't kept patched.

Objective: 1.3 Distinguish and differentiate network design elements and compounds

35. An organization wants to hide addresses it uses on its internal network. What can assist with this goal?

    A. MAC filtering

    B. NAC

    C. NAT

    D. DMZ

36. **C** is correct. Network Address Translation (NAT) translates public IP addresses to private, private IP addresses back to public, and hides addresses on the internal network.

A is incorrect. Port security and network access control use MAC filtering to limit access.

B is incorrect. Network access control can inspect clients for health prior to allowing network access.

D is incorrect. A DMZ provides access to services (hosted on servers) from the Internet while providing a layer of protection for the internal network.

Objective: 1.3 Distinguish and differentiate network design elements and compounds

36. What type of attack starts on a virtual system but can affect the physical host?

    A. TPM

    B. DLP

    C. VM escape

    D. VMware

36. **C** is correct. A VM escape attack runs on a virtual system and if successful, allows the attacker to control the physical host server and all other virtual servers on the physical server.

A is incorrect. A TPM is a hardware chip that stores encryption keys and provides full disk encryption.

B is incorrect. A DLP is a device that reduces the risk of employees emailing confidential information outside the organization.

D is incorrect. VMware is a popular virtualization application.

Objective: 1.3 Distinguish and differentiate network design elements and compounds

37. Which of the following protocols is a file transfer protocol using SSH?

    A. SFTP

    B. TFTP

    C. SICMP

    D. CCMP

37. **A** is correct. Secure FTP (SFTP) is a secure implementation of FTP, an extension of Secure Shell (SSH), and it transmits data using port 22.

B is incorrect. Trivial FTP is a form of FTP using UDP to transmit smaller amounts of data than FTP.

C is incorrect. ICMP is a diagnostic protocol used by tools such as ping, but there is no such thing as SICMP.

D is incorrect. CCMP is an encryption protocol used with wireless networks.

Objective: 1.4 Implement and use common protocols

38. Of the following choices, which one provides the most security for FTP?

    A. FTP active mode

    B. FTPS

    C. TFTP

    D. SCP

38. **B** is correct. File Transfer Protocol Secure (FTPS) uses SSL to secure FTP transmissions.

A is incorrect. FTP can work in active or passive mode but this only affects how the ports are used, not the security.

C is incorrect. TFTP is a trivial form of FTP and doesn't provide security.

D is incorrect. SCP uses SSH to copy files over a network and isn't related to FTP.

Objective: 1.4 Implement and use common protocols

39. Of the following choices, what is a benefit of IPsec?

    A. MAC filtering

    B. Flood guard

    C. Load balancing

    D. Payload encryption

39. **D** is correct. Internet Protocol security (IPsec) includes Encapsulating Security Payload (ESP), which can encrypt the IP packet payload.

A is incorrect. Port security and network access control can use MAC filtering.

B and C are incorrect. A flood guard protects against SYN flood attacks and a load balancer can optimize and distribute data loads across multiple computers, but neither are related to IPsec.

Objective: 1.4 Implement and use common protocols

40. What protocol is used to monitor and configure network devices?

    A. ICMP

    B. SFTP

    C. SNMP

    D. DNS

40. **C** is correct. Simple Network Management Protocol (SNMP) can monitor and manage network devices such as routers or switches and uses device traps.

A is incorrect. Diagnostic tools such as ping use ICMP and many firewalls block ICMP traffic.

B is incorrect. SFTP is a secure form of FTP used to upload and download files.

D is incorrect. DNS resolves host names to IP addresses.

Objective: 1.4 Implement and use common protocols

41. Which of the following is an IPv6 address?

    A. 192.168.1.100

    B. 192.168.1.100 /128

    C. FE80:20D4:3FF7:003F:DE62

    D. FE80:0000:0000:0000:20D4:3FF7:003F:DE62

41. **D** is correct. An IPv6 address uses 128-bit IP addresses and includes eight groups of four hexadecimal characters.

A and B are incorrect. IPv4 (not IPv6) uses the dotted decimal format with decimals separated by dots.

C is incorrect. A double colon indicates zero compression, when less than eight groups are shown, but if omitted the address isn't valid.

Objective: 1.4 Implement and use common protocols

42. An administrator decides to block Telnet access to an internal network from any remote device on the Internet. Which of the following is the best choice to accomplish this?

    A. Block port 22 at the host firewall

    B. Block port 22 on internal routers

    C. Block port 23 at the network firewall

    D. Block port 23 on internal routers

42. **C** is correct. You can block all telnet traffic into the network by blocking port 23 on the network firewall.

A and B are incorrect. Port 22 is used for SSH, SCP or SFTP, not Telnet (unless Telnet is encrypted with SSH). Additionally, blocking it at the host firewall only blocks it to the host, not the network.

D is incorrect. It's easier to block the port once at the firewall rather than block the port on all internal routers. Additionally, the scenario states that the goal is to block access from the Internet, but Telnet may be authorized internally.

Objective: 1.5 Identify commonly used default network ports

43. What port does SFTP use?

      A. 22

      B. 23

      C. 443

      D. 1443

43. **A** is correct. Secure File Transfer Protocol (SFTP) uses port 22, as do other protocols encrypted with Secure Shell (SSH) such as Secure Copy (SCP).

B is incorrect. Telnet uses port 23.

C is incorrect. HTTPS uses port 443.

D is incorrect. Microsoft's SQL Server uses port 1443.

Objective: 1.5 Identify commonly used default network ports

44. What ports do HTTP and HTTPS use?

    A. 20 and 21

    B. 22 and 25

    C. 80 and 443

    D. 80 and 1433

44. **C** is correct. Hypertext Transfer Protocol (HTTP) uses port 80 and HTTP Secure (HTTPS) uses port 443, and they are both used to transfer web pages.

A is incorrect. FTP uses ports 20 and 21.

B is incorrect. Microsoft's SQL server uses port 1433.

D is incorrect. SFTP and SCP use port 22. SMTP uses port 25.

Objective: 1.5 Identify commonly used default network ports

45. What port does SMTP use?

    A. 22

    B. 25

    C. 110

    D. 143

45. **B** is correct. Simple Mail Transfer Protocol (SMTP) uses port 25.

A is incorrect. SCP, TFTP, and SSH all use port 22.

C is incorrect. POP3 uses port 110.

D is incorrect. IMAP4 uses port 143.

Objective: 1.5 Identify commonly used default network ports

46. Of the following choices, what ports are used by NetBIOS? (Choose two.)

    A. 80

    B. 137

    C. 139

    D. 3389

46. **B** and **C** are correct. NetBIOS uses ports 137, 138, and 139. A and D are incorrect. HTTP uses port 80 and remote desktop services uses port 3389.

Objective: 1.5 Identify commonly used default network ports

47. You've recently completed a wireless audit and realize that the wireless signal from your company's WAP reaches the parking lot. What can you do to ensure that the signal doesn't reach outside your building?

    A. Increase the WAP's power level

    B. Decrease the WAP's power level

    C. Enable SSID broadcasting

    D. Disable SSID broadcasting

47. **B** is correct. You can decrease the wireless access point's (WAP's) power level to reduce the footprint and ensure the WAP's signal doesn't reach outside the parking lot (or reposition the WAP's antenna).

A is incorrect. Increasing the WAP's power level increases the footprint.

C and D are incorrect. SSID broadcasting won't have an impact on the footprint.

Objective: 1.6 Implement wireless network in a secure manner

48. Your organization is designing an 802.11n network and they want to use the strongest security. What would you recommend?

    A. FTPS

    B. SSL

    C. WEP

    D. WPA2

48. **D** is correct. Wi-Fi Protected Access version 2 (WPA2) provides the strongest security for an 802.11n (wireless) network of the given choices.

A is incorrect. FTPS secures FTP traffic with SSL.

B is incorrect. SSL encrypts other types of traffic, but not wireless network traffic.

C is incorrect. WEP is weak and should not be used.

Objective: 1.6 Implement wireless network in a secure manner

49. Which of the following authentication mechanisms can provide centralized authentication for a wireless network?

    A. WPA2

    B. RADIUS

    C. Multifactor authentication

    D. Kerberos

49. **B** is correct. Remote Authentication Dial-in user Service (RADIUS) can provide centralized authentication for wireless networks as an 802.1X server in Enterprise mode.

A is incorrect. WPA2 provides security for a wireless network.

C is incorrect. Multifactor authentication uses two or more factors of authentication but does not provide centralized authentication.

D is incorrect. Kerberos provides authentication in Microsoft networks.

Objective: 1.6 Implement wireless network in a secure manner

50. You want to ensure that only specific wireless clients can access your wireless networks. Of the following choices, what provides the best solution?

    A. MAC filtering

    B. Content filtering

    C. NAT

    D. NIPS

50. **A** is correct. MAC filtering allows you to restrict access to the wireless networks to devices with specified MAC addresses (though an attacker can circumvent this method).

B is incorrect. Content filtering can filter traffic for malware and more, but it doesn't restrict clients.

C is incorrect. NAT translates IP addresses and can hide internal private IP addresses but it doesn't restrict access.

D is incorrect. NIPS can detect and block attacks, but not filter wireless clients.

Objective: 1.6 Implement wireless network in a secure manner

51. You recently completed a wireless audit of your company's wireless network. You've identified several unknown devices connected to the network and realize they are devices owned by company employees. What can you use to prevent these devices from connecting?

    A. MAC filtering

    B. Enable SSID broadcast

    C. Enable isolation mode on the WAP

    D. Reduce the power levels on the WAP

51. **A** is correct. MAC filtering can restrict the devices connectivity based on their MAC address, and prevent the employees devices from connecting.

B is incorrect. Enabling SSID broadcast won't prevent the devices from connecting.

C is incorrect. Isolation mode prevents wireless users from connecting to each other, not the WAP.

D is incorrect. Reducing the power levels reduces access for all devices, not just the employee owned devices.

Objective: 1.6 Implement wireless network in a secure manner

52. What can you do to prevent the easy discovery of a WAP?

    A. Enable MAC filtering

    B. Disable SSID broadcast

    C. Enable SSID broadcast

    D. Enable 802.1X authentication

52. **B** is correct. You can disable SSID broadcasts to prevent the easy discovery of a WAP but attackers can still locate the wireless network with a sniffer.

A is incorrect. MAC filtering can restrict what devices can connect, but attackers can circumvent this method too.

C is incorrect. Enabling the SSID broadcast makes the WAP easier to discover.

D is incorrect. 802.1X authentication uses a RADIUS server to add security, but doesn't prevent the easy discovery of a WAP.

Objective: 1.6 Implement wireless network in a secure manner

Chapter 2 Compliance and Operational Security

Compliance and Operational Security topics are **18 percent** of the CompTIA Security+ exam. The objectives in this domain are:

2.1 Explain risk related concepts
- Control types
  - o Technical
  - o Management
  - o Operational
- False positives
- Importance of policies in reducing risk
  - o Privacy policy
  - o Acceptable use
  - o Security policy
  - o Mandatory vacations
  - o Job rotation
  - o Separation of duties
  - o Least privilege
- Risk calculation
  - o Likelihood
  - o ALE
  - o Impact
- Quantitative vs. qualitative
- Risk-avoidance, transference, acceptance, mitigation, deterrence
- Risks associated to Cloud Computing and Virtualization

2.2 Carry out appropriate risk mitigation strategies
- Implement security controls based on risk
- Change management
- Incident management
- User rights and permissions reviews

- Perform routine audits
- Implement policies and procedures to prevent data loss or theft

2.3 Execute appropriate incident response procedures
- Basic forensic procedures
  - Order of volatility
  - Capture system image
  - Network traffic and logs
  - Capture video
  - Record time offset
  - Take hashes
  - Screenshots
  - Witnesses
  - Track man hours and expense
- Damage and loss control
- Chain of custody
- Incident response: first responder

2.4 Explain the importance of security related awareness and training
- Security policy training and procedures
- Personally identifiable information
- Information classification: Sensitivity of data (hard or soft)
- Data labeling, handling and disposal
- Compliance with laws, best practices and standards
- User habits
  - Password behaviors
  - Data handling
  - Clean desk policies
  - Prevent tailgating
  - Personally owned devices
- Threat awareness
  - New viruses)
  - Phishing attacks
  - Zero days exploits
- Use of social networking and P2P

2.5 Compare and contrast aspects of business continuity
- Business impact analysis
- Removing single points of failure
- Business continuity planning and testing
- Continuity of operations
- Disaster recovery
- IT contingency planning
- Succession planning

2.6 Explain the impact and proper use of environmental controls
- HVAC
- Fire suppression
- EMI shielding
- Hot and cold aisles
- Environmental monitoring
- Temperature and humidity controls
- Video monitoring

2.7 Execute disaster recovery plans and procedures
- Backup / backout contingency plans or policies
- Backups, execution and frequency
- Redundancy and fault tolerance
    o Hardware
    o RAID
    o Clustering
    o Load balancing
    o Servers
- High availability
- Cold site, hot site, warm site
- Mean time to restore, mean time between failures, recovery time objectives and recovery point objectives

2.8 Exemplify the concepts of confidentiality, integrity and availability (CIA)

The CompTIA Security+: Get Certified Get Ahead SY0-301 Study Guide (ISBN 1463762364) discusses these topics in much more depth. Sec-plus.com has more details on the availability of this book.

√ **Get Certified**
√ **Get Ahead**

Practice Test Questions for
Compliance and Operational Security Domain

1. Of the following choices, what type of control is least privilege?

    A. Corrective

    B. Technical

    C. Detective

    D. Preventative

2. Of the following choices, what type of control is a vulnerability assessment?

    A. Corrective

    B. Management

    C. Detective

    D. Technical

3. What policy informs users of proper system usage?

    A. Acceptable use policy

    B. Clean desk policy

    C. Data labeling policy

    D. Data classification policy

4. Employees in the accounting department are forced to take time off from their duties on a regular basis. What would direct this?

    A. Account disablement policy

    B. Mandatory vacation policy

C. Job rotation policy

D. Dual accounts for administrators

5. Two administrators within an organization perform different functions and have different privileges. They are required to swap roles annually. What policy would direct this?

A. Mandatory vacation policy

B. Separation of duties policy

C. Least privilege policy

D. Job rotation policy

6. A group of server administrators maintains several database servers, but they cannot access security logs on these servers. Security administrators can access the security logs, but they cannot access data within the databases. What policy is the company using?

A. Separation of duties policy

B. Policy requiring dual accounts for administrators

C. Job rotation policy

D. Mandatory vacations policy

7. Your company has a public web site. Where could you identify what data is collected from users on this web site?

A. PII policy

B. Privacy policy

C. Clean desk policy

D. Data retention policy

8. An organization has purchased fire insurance to manage the risk of a potential fire. What method are they using?

    A. Risk acceptance

    B. Risk avoidance

    C. Risk deterrence

    D. Risk mitigation

    E. Risk transference

9. What is the purpose of risk mitigation?

    A. Reduce the chances that a threat will exploit a vulnerability

    B. Reduce the chances that a vulnerability will exploit a threat

    C. Eliminate risk

    D. Eliminate threats

10. Of the following choices, what best identifies the purpose of a change management program?

    A. It defines the process and accounting structure for handling system modifications

    B. It provides a method of defining a timeline for installing patches

    C. It is a primary method of protecting against loss of confidentiality

    D. It reduces the footprint of a datacenter

11. Your organization wants to prevent unintended outages caused from changes to systems. What could they use?

    A. Patch management

B. Regression testing

C. Change management

D. Security template

12. Of the following choices, what is an example of a system audit?

A. Separation of duties

B. User rights and permissions review

C. Whaling

D. Smurf review

13. After a recent security incident, a security administrator discovered someone used an enabled account of an ex-employee to access data in the Sales department. What should be done to prevent this in the future?

A. Modify the security policy to disable all accounts in the Sales department

B. Vulnerability scans

C. Port scans

D. User access review

14. An administrator recently discovered an active attack on a database server. The server hosts customer PII and other data. What should the administrator do first?

A. Create a chain of custody

B. Create an image of the memory

C. Disconnect the server from the network

D. Create an image of the disks

15. Of the following choices, what is a likely response to a security breach?

    A. Backup data

    B. Begin a forensic evaluation

    C. Enable a NIDS

    D. Encrypt data with AES-128

16. Investigators suspect that an internal computer was involved in an attack but the computer has been turned off. What information is unavailable for an investigation? (Choose all that apply).

    A. Memory

    B. Network processes

    C. Files

    D. System processes

    E. Master boot record

17. What should a forensics expert do before analyzing a hard drive for evidence?

    A. Create a listing of files

    B. Identify the last file opened on the system

    C. Create an image of the system memory

    D. Image the drive

18. A forensic expert collected a laptop as evidence. What provides assurances that the system was properly handled while it was transported?

    A. System log

    B. Security log

    C. Chain of custody

    D. Forensic hash

19. A forensic expert created an image copy of a hard drive and created a chain of custody. What does the chain of custody provide?

    A. Confidentiality of the original data

    B. Documentation on who handled the evidence

    C. Verification of integrity with a hash

    D. Proof that the image wasn't modified

20. An organization wants to reduce the possibility of data theft. Of the following choices, what can assist with this goal?

    A. Requiring the use of USB thumb drives to store data

    B. Removing DLP devices

    C. Store copies of the data in the cloud

    D. Clean desk policy

21. A company provides employees with annual security awareness training. Of the following choices, what is the most likely reason the company is doing this?

    A. To increase the number of security incidents

    B. To educate users about changes in the IT network

C. To eliminate malware attacks

D. To reinforce user compliance with security policies

22. A company is creating a security awareness and training plan for employees. Of the following choices, what will affect its success the most?

A. Support from senior management

B. Acceptance by employees

C. Technical controls used

D. Method of training

23. An organization is not actively involved in business continuity planning. What are they likely to overlook until a disaster results in a major outage.

A. Data encryption

B. Single points of failure

C. Vulnerability scans

D. Penetration tests

24. Of the following choices, what identifies RPOs and RTOs?

A. Failover clusters

B. BIA

C. RAID

D. DRP

25. An organization is creating a business continuity plan (BCP). What will identify business requirements used in the development of the plan?

    A. BIA

    B. RPO

    C. RTO

    D. HSM

26. How can an organization validate a BCP?

    A. With a BIA

    B. With a hot site

    C. With testing

    D. With a hierarchical list of critical systems

27. Your organization is addressing single points of failure as potential risks to security. What are they addressing?

    A. Confidentiality

    B. Integrity

    C. Availability

    D. Authentication

28. An organization hosts several bays of servers used to support a large online ecommerce business. Which one of the following choices would increase the availability of this datacenter?

    A. Encryption

    B. Hashing

    C. Generators

D. Integrity

29. Your building is researching the costs and functionality of fire alarm systems for a new building. What capability should the system include to prevent a fire from spreading?

    A. Integration with a temperature control system

    B. Integration with a CCTV

    C. Integration with an HVAC system

    D. Integration with proximity card readers

30. An organization designed their datacenter with hot and cold aisles. Of the following choices, what is not a valid purpose of hot and cold aisles?

    A. Regulate cooling

    B. Increase availability

    C. Reduce cooling costs

    D. Fire suppression

31. Your organization hosts several bays of servers within a server room. What environmental control within the datacenter requires a thermostat?

    A. Temperature control

    B. Hot and cold aisles

    C. Humidity control

    D. Generators

32. An organization hosts several bays of servers used to support a large online ecommerce business. They want to ensure that customer data hosted within the datacenter is protected and they implement several access controls including an HVAC system. What does this the HVAC system help protect?

    A. Access

    B. Availability

    C. Confidentiality

    D. Integrity

33. Of the following choices, what is the best choice to help prevent someone from capturing network traffic?

    A. EMI shielding

    B. Use hubs instead of switches

    C. Ensure that SNMP traps are set

    D. Hot and cold aisles

34. Which of the following provides fault tolerance through disk mirroring?

    A. RAID-0

    B. RAID-1

    C. RAID-5

    D. Clustering

35. An administrator is improving the availability of a server and needs to ensure that a hard drive failure does not result in the failure of the server. What will support this goal? (Choose all that apply.)

A. Hardware RAID-0

B. Hardware RAID-1

C. Software RAID-1

D. Software RAID-5

36. What can remove a server as a single point of failure?

A. RAID-1

B. Mirroring

C. Clustering

D. UPS

37. Several servers in your server room are connected to an UPS. What does this provide?

A. Continuity of operations

B. Disaster recovery

C. Fault tolerance

D. Long term power if commercial power fails

38. What helps ensure availability in the event of an extended power outage?

A. UPS

B. Failover clusters

C. RAID

D. Generators

39. You need to implement a backup strategy that allows the fastest recovery of data. What provides the best solution?

A. A full backup daily

B. A full/differential strategy

C. A full/incremental strategy

D. A differential/incremental strategy

40. An organization regularly performs backups of critical systems. Where should they keep a copy of the backups for retention?

A. Off-site

B. With the backed up systems

C. On a mirrored drive of the backed up system

D. On a cluster

41. An organization wants to verify that a tape backup can be restored in its entirety. What should they do?

A. Perform test restores of random files on the backup

B. Perform test restores of the full backup

C. Copy the backup to the hot site

D. Copy the backup to the cold site

42. A business impact analysis (BIA) determined that a critical business function has a Recovery Time Objective (RTO) of an hour. What site will meet this objective?

A. Hot site

B. Cold site

C. Warm site

D. RTO site

43. Which of the following continuity of operations solutions is the most expensive?

    A. Hot site

    B. Cold site

    C. Warm site

    D. Clustered site

44. An organization is considering an alternate location as part of their business continuity plan. They want to identify a solution that provides a balance between cost and recovery time. What will they choose?

    A. Hot site

    B. Cold site

    C. Warm site

    D. Mirrored site

45. Of the following choices, what is needed in a cold site used for continuity of operations?

    A. Power and connectivity

    B. All required equipment

    C. All required equipment with up-to-date patches

    D. All required equipment with up-to-date patches and data

46. An organization is performing a disaster recovery exercise. Of the following choices, what is likely to be included?

    A. Test server restoration

    B. Picking a hot, warm, or cold site

    C. Creation of BIA

D. Determination of the failsafe state

47. An organization implemented a disaster recovery plan in response to a hurricane. What is the last step in the disaster recovery process?

    A. Activation

    B. Recover systems

    C. Test systems

    D. Review

48. An administrator used a disaster recovery plan to rebuild a critical server after an attack. Of the following choices, how can the administrator verify the system's functionality?

    A. Perform a review of the recovery process

    B. Install approved changes

    C. Compare the system's performance against a performance baseline

    D. Removed antivirus software

49. A critical system failed. Of the following choices, what would an organization implement to restore it?

    A. BIA

    B. DRP

    C. COOP

    D. RAID

50. A database administrator is tasked with increasing the retail prices of all products in a database by 10 percent. The administrator writes a script performing a bulk update of the database and executes it. However, all retail prices are doubled (increased by 100 percent instead of 10 percent). What has been lost?

    A. Confidentiality

    B. Integrity

    C. Hashing

    D. Authentication

51. You want to ensure that data has not been changed between the time when it was sent and when it arrived at its destination. What provides this assurance?

    A. Confidentiality

    B. Integrity

    C. Availability

    D. Authentication

52. You are planning to host a free online forum for users to share IT security related information with each other. Any user can anonymously view data. They can post messages after logging in but you do not want them to be able modify other user's posts. What levels of confidentiality, integrity, and availability should you seek?

    A. Low confidentiality, low integrity, and low availability

    B. Medium confidentiality, low integrity, and high availability

    C. High confidentiality, low integrity, and low availability

D. Low confidentiality, medium integrity, and medium availability

53. You want to ensure that data is only viewable by authorized users. What security principle are you trying to enforce?

    A. Confidentiality

    B. Integrity

    C. Availability

    D. Authentication

Practice Test Questions with Answers for Compliance and Operational Security Domain

1. Of the following choices, what type of control is least privilege?

    A. Corrective

    B. Technical

    C. Detective

    D. Preventative

1. **B** is correct. The principle of least privilege is a technical control and ensures that users only have the rights and permissions needed to perform the job, and no more.

A is incorrect. A corrective control attempts to reverse the effects of a problem.

C is incorrect. A detective control (such as a security audit) detects when a vulnerability has been exploited.

D is incorrect. A preventative control attempts to prevent an incident from occurring.

Objective: 2.1 Explain risk related concepts

2. Of the following choices, what type of control is a vulnerability assessment?

    A. Corrective

    B. Management

    C. Detective

    D. Technical

2. **B** is correct. A vulnerability assessment is a management control and attempts to discover weaknesses in systems.

A is incorrect. A corrective control attempts to reverse the effects of a problem.

C is incorrect. A detective control (such as a security audit) detects when a vulnerability has been exploited.

D is incorrect. A technical control (such as the principle of least privilege) enforces security using technical means.

Objective: 2.1 Explain risk related concepts

3. What policy informs users of proper system usage?

    A. Acceptable use policy

    B. Clean desk policy

    C. Data labeling policy

    D. Data classification policy

3. **A** is correct. An acceptable use policy defines proper system usage for users.

B is incorrect. A clean desk policy requires users to organize their areas to reduce the risk of possible data theft and password compromise.

C and D are incorrect. Data labeling and classification policies help users understand the value of data and data labeling ensures that users know what data they are handling and processing.

Objective: 2.1 Explain risk related concepts

4. Employees in the accounting department are forced to take time off from their duties on a regular basis. What would direct this?

    A. Account disablement policy

    B. Mandatory vacation policy

    C. Job rotation policy

    D. Dual accounts for administrators

4. **B** is correct. Mandatory vacation policies require employees to take time away from their job and help to detect fraud or malicious activities.

A is incorrect. An account disablement policy (sometimes called an account expiration policy) specifies when to disable accounts.

C is incorrect. Job rotation policies require employees to change roles on a regular basis.

D is incorrect. Dual accounts for administrators help prevent privilege escalation attacks.

Objective: 2.1 Explain risk related concepts

5. Two administrators within an organization perform different functions and have different privileges. They are required to swap roles annually. What policy would direct this?

    A. Mandatory vacation policy

    B. Separation of duties policy

    C. Least privilege policy

    D. Job rotation policy

5. **D** is correct. Job rotation policies require employees to change roles on a regular basis.

A is incorrect. Mandatory vacation policies require employees to take time away from their job and help detect malicious activities.

B is incorrect. A separation of duties policy separates individual tasks of an overall function between different people.

C is incorrect. Least privilege ensures that users are granted only the rights and permissions needed to perform assigned tasks but doesn't require swapping roles.

Objective: 2.1 Explain risk related concepts

6. A group of server administrators maintains several database servers, but they cannot access security logs on these servers. Security administrators can access the security logs, but they cannot access data within the databases. What policy is the company using?

    A. Separation of duties policy

    B. Policy requiring dual accounts for administrators

    C. Job rotation policy

    D. Mandatory vacations policy

6. **A** is correct. A separation of duties policy separates individual tasks of an overall function between different people and in this case, it is separating maintenance of the database servers with security oversight of the servers.

B is incorrect. Dual accounts for administrators (one for administrative use and one for regular use) help prevent privilege escalation attacks.

C is incorrect. Job rotation policies require employees to change roles on a regular basis.

D is incorrect. Mandatory vacation policies require employees to take time away from their job and help detect malicious activities.

Objective: 2.1 Explain risk related concepts

7. Your company has a public web site. Where could you identify what data is collected from users on this web site?

    A. PII policy

    B. Privacy policy

    C. Clean desk policy

    D. Data retention policy

7. **B** is correct. A privacy policy identifies what data is collected from users on a web site.

A is incorrect. A PII policy identifies procedures for handling and retaining PII but wouldn't necessarily identify data collected from a web site.

C is incorrect. A clean desk policy requires users to organize their areas to reduce the risk of possible data theft and password compromise.

D is incorrect. A data retention policy identifies how long to keep data.

Objective: 2.1 Explain risk related concepts

8. An organization has purchased fire insurance to manage the risk of a potential fire. What method are they using?

    A. Risk acceptance

    B. Risk avoidance

C. Risk deterrence

D. Risk mitigation

E. Risk transference

8. **E is correct.** Purchasing insurance is a common method of risk transference.

A is incorrect. Organizations often accept a risk when the cost of the control exceeds the cost of the risk.

B is incorrect. An organization can avoid a risk by not providing a service or participating in a risky activity.

C is incorrect. Risk deterrence attempts to discourage attacks with preventative controls such as a security guard.

D is incorrect. Risk mitigation reduces risks through internal controls.

Objective: 2.1 Explain risk related concepts

9. What is the purpose of risk mitigation?

    A. Reduce the chances that a threat will exploit a vulnerability

    B. Reduce the chances that a vulnerability will exploit a threat

    C. Eliminate risk

    D. Eliminate threats

9. **A is correct.** Risk mitigation reduces the chances that a threat will exploit a vulnerability.

B is incorrect. Risk is the likelihood that a threat (such as an attacker) will exploit a vulnerability (any weakness). A vulnerability cannot exploit a threat.

C and D are incorrect. You cannot eliminate risk or eliminate threats.

Objective: 2.1 Explain risk related concepts

10. Of the following choices, what best identifies the purpose of a change management program?

    A. It defines the process and accounting structure for handling system modifications

    B. It provides a method of defining a timeline for installing patches

    C. It is a primary method of protecting against loss of confidentiality

    D. It reduces the footprint of a datacenter

10. **A** is correct. A change management system defines the process and accounting structure for system modifications.

B is incorrect. A patch management policy defines a timeline for installing patches, but change management isn't restricted to only applying patches.

C is incorrect. Encryption and access controls protect against loss of confidentiality.

D is incorrect. Virtualization and cloud computing can reduce the footprint of a data center.

Objective: 2.2 Carry out appropriate risk mitigation strategies

11. Your organization wants to prevent unintended outages caused from changes to systems. What could they use?

    A. Patch management

    B. Regression testing

C. Change management

D. Security template

11. **C** is correct. A change management system helps prevent unintended outages from unauthorized changes, and provides a method of documenting all changes.

A is incorrect. Patch management ensures that systems are up-to-date with current patches.

B is incorrect. Regression testing verifies that a patch has not introduced new errors.

D is incorrect. You can use security templates to deploy multiple systems using the same settings.

Objective: 2.2 Carry out appropriate risk mitigation strategies

12. Of the following choices, what is an example of a system audit?

    A. Separation of duties

    B. User rights and permissions review

    C. Whaling

    D. Smurf review

12. **B** is correct. Reviewing user rights and permissions is an example of a system audit.

A is incorrect. Separation of duties prevents any one person or entity from completing all the functions of a critical or sensitive process, and helps to prevent fraud, theft, and errors.

C is incorrect. Whaling is a form of phishing that targets high-level executives.

D is incorrect. Smurf is a type of attack that can be detected with a NIDS.

Objective: 2.2 Carry out appropriate risk mitigation strategies

13. After a recent security incident, a security administrator discovered someone used an enabled account of an ex-employee to access data in the Sales department. What should be done to prevent this in the future?

    A. Modify the security policy to disable all accounts in the Sales department

    B. Vulnerability scans

    C. Port scans

    D. User access review

13. **D** is correct. A user rights and access review will detect inactive accounts and accounts with more permissions than they require.

A is incorrect. Normally, a security policy will direct that accounts are disabled or deleted when an employee leaves, but isn't appropriate to disable all accounts for a department.

B and C are incorrect. Neither vulnerability scans nor port scans can detect if an account is for a current or previous employee.

Objective: 2.2 Carry out appropriate risk mitigation strategies

14. An administrator recently discovered an active attack on a database server. The server hosts customer PII and other data. What should the administrator do first?

    A. Create a chain of custody

B. Create an image of the memory

C. Disconnect the server from the network

D. Create an image of the disks

14. **C** is correct. Containment is an important first step after verifying an incident and disconnecting the server will contain this incident.

A, B, and D are incorrect. A chain of custody provides assurances that evidence (such as memory or disk images) has been controlled and handled properly after collection, but this isn't done before containing the problem.

Objective: 2.3 Execute appropriate incident response procedures

15. Of the following choices, what is a likely response to a security breach?

A. Backup data

B. Begin a forensic evaluation

C. Enable a NIDS

D. Encrypt data with AES-128

15. **B** is correct. Once an organization identifies an incident and contains it, they will begin a forensic evaluation.

A is incorrect. It's too late to backup data *after* a breach.

C is incorrect. A network intrusion detection system (NIDS) can detect attacks, but a NIDS should be running at all times, not just after a breach.

D is incorrect. Encryption of data with AES-128 will protect confidentiality but it won't help after the breach.

Objective: 2.3 Execute appropriate incident response procedures

16. Investigators suspect that an internal computer was involved in an attack but the computer has been turned off. What information is unavailable for an investigation? (Choose all that apply).

> A. Memory

> B. Network processes

> C. Files

> D. System processes

> E. Master boot record

16. **A, B, D** are correct. Data in memory is volatile and not available after turning a system off. Additionally, any processes or applications are not running when the system is powered off since this information is stored in volatile memory.

C and E are incorrect. Files are stored on disks and disk data (including the master boot record) remains available even after turning off power to the system.

Objective: 2.3 Execute appropriate incident response procedures

17. What should a forensics expert do before analyzing a hard drive for evidence?

> A. Create a listing of files

> B. Identify the last file opened on the system

> C. Create an image of the system memory

> D. Image the drive

17. **D** is correct. Hard drive imaging creates a forensic copy and prevents the forensic analysis from modifying the original evidence.

A and B are incorrect. Listing or identifying files is part of analysis and should not be done before an image is created.

C is incorrect. It's valuable to create an image of system memory before powering down a system, but this is unrelated to analyzing a hard drive.

Objective: 2.3 Execute appropriate incident response procedures

18. A forensic expert collected a laptop as evidence. What provides assurances that the system was properly handled while it was transported?

    A. System log

    B. Security log

    C. Chain of custody

    D. Forensic hash

18. **C** is correct. A chain of custody provides assurances that evidence has been controlled and handled properly after collection.

A and B are incorrect. The System log records system events such as when a service stops and starts and the Security log records auditable events such as user logons and logoffs, but neither document transportation.

D is incorrect. A forensic hash provides assurances that an image or file has not been modified.

Objective: 2.3 Execute appropriate incident response procedures

19. A forensic expert created an image copy of a hard drive and created a chain of custody. What does the chain of custody provide?

    A. Confidentiality of the original data

    B. Documentation on who handled the evidence

    C. Verification of integrity with a hash

    D. Proof that the image wasn't modified

19. **B** is correct. A chain of custody provides assurances that evidence has been controlled and documents who handled the evidence.

A is incorrect. Confidentiality is provided with encryption, not a chain of custody.

C and D are incorrect. The expert may create a hash before and after capturing the image to prove the image wasn't modified, but this provides integrity and is not related to a chain of custody.

Objective: 2.3 Execute appropriate incident response procedures

20. An organization wants to reduce the possibility of data theft. Of the following choices, what can assist with this goal?

    A. Requiring the use of USB thumb drives to store data

    B. Removing DLP devices

    C. Store copies of the data in the cloud

    D. Clean desk policy

20. **D** is correct. A clean desk policy requires users to organize their areas to reduce the risk of possible data theft and password compromise.

A is incorrect. USB thumb drives increase the risk of data theft and data leakage.

B is incorrect. Data Loss Prevention (DLP) devices such as network-based DLPs can detect data leakage.

C is incorrect. Because cloud computing stores data in unknown locations accessible via the Internet, you lose physical control of the data.

Objective: 2.4 Explain the importance of security related awareness and training

21. A company provides employees with annual security awareness training. Of the following choices, what is the most likely reason the company is doing this?

    A. To increase the number of security incidents

    B. To educate users about changes in the IT network

    C. To eliminate malware attacks

    D. To reinforce user compliance with security policies

21. **D** is correct. Organizations provide security awareness training to reinforce user compliance with security policies and to minimize the risk posed by users.

A is incorrect. The goal is to reduce, not increase, the number of incidents.

B is incorrect. End users don't need to be educated about the IT network, but an acceptable use policy does educate them about proper system usage.

C is incorrect. Training may educate users about malware, but it's not possible to eliminate all malware attacks.

Objective: 2.4 Explain the importance of security related awareness and training

22. A company is creating a security awareness and training plan for employees. Of the following choices, what will affect its success the most?

    A. Support from senior management

    B. Acceptance by employees

    C. Technical controls used

    D. Method of training

22. **A** is correct. The success of a security education and awareness plan is directly related to the amount of support from senior management.

B is incorrect. If senior management supports the plan, employees will accept it.

C is incorrect. Technical controls (such as a firewall) enforce security but are not typically included in a security awareness and training plan.

D is incorrect. Multiple methods of training and different environments require different methods.

Objective: 2.4 Explain the importance of security related awareness and training

23. An organization is not actively involved in business continuity planning. What are they likely to overlook until a disaster results in a major outage.

    A. Data encryption

    B. Single points of failure

    C. Vulnerability scans

    D. Penetration tests

23. **B** is correct. Single points of failure are often overlooked until a disaster occurs.

A, C, and D are incorrect. Business continuity planning helps an organization plan for disasters and continuity of operations but it does not include data encryption, vulnerability scans, or penetration tests.

Objective: 2.5 Compare and contrast aspects of business continuity

24. Of the following choices, what identifies RPOs and RTOs?

    A. Failover clusters

    B. BIA

    C. RAID

    D. DRP

24. **B** is correct. A business impact analysis (BIA) identifies the Recovery Point Objectives (RPOs) and Recovery Time Objectives (RTOs).

A and C are incorrect. Failover clusters reduce the likelihood of a single point of failure when a server fails and a Redundant Array of Independent Disks (RAID) increases availability for hard drives.

D is incorrect. A disaster recovery plan (DRP) helps an organization prepare for potential disasters and includes a hierarchical list of critical systems.

Objective: 2.5 Compare and contrast aspects of business continuity

25. An organization is creating a business continuity plan (BCP). What will identify business requirements used in the development of the plan?

    A. BIA

    B. RPO

    C. RTO

    D. HSM

25. **A** is correct. A business impact analysis (BIA) identifies critical business functions and requirements and is created as part of the BCP.

B and C are incorrect. Recovery Point Objectives (RPOs) and Recovery Time Objectives (RTOs) are part of the BIA.

D is incorrect. A hardware security module (HSM) is a removable or external device that provides encryption services but it does not identify security requirements.

Objective: 2.5 Compare and contrast aspects of business continuity

26. How can an organization validate a BCP?

    A. With a BIA

    B. With a hot site

    C. With testing

    D. With a hierarchical list of critical systems

26. **C** is correct. Business continuity plans (BCPs) and disaster recovery plans (DRPs) are validated through testing such as an annual or semi-annual test.

A is incorrect. A business impact analysis (BIA) identifies critical business functions using elements such as Recovery Point Objectives and Recovery Time Objectives.

B is incorrect. A hot site is an alternate location ready for operation within an hour but not all BCPs require alternate locations.

D is incorrect. A DRP will include a hierarchical list of critical systems but the list doesn't validate a BCP.

Objective: 2.5 Compare and contrast aspects of business continuity

27. Your organization is addressing single points of failure as potential risks to security. What are they addressing?

    A. Confidentiality

    B. Integrity

    C. Availability

    D. Authentication

27. **C** is correct. By addressing a single point of failure (SPOF), you increase availability. An SPOF can be a drive, a server, power, cooling or any other item whose failure will cause the entire system to fail.

A and B are incorrect. Confidentiality is enforced with encryption, and integrity is enforced with hashing,

D is incorrect. Authentication provides proof of a user's identity.

Objective: 2.5 Compare and contrast aspects of business continuity

28. An organization hosts several bays of servers used to support a large online ecommerce business. Which one of the following choices would increase the availability of this datacenter?

    A. Encryption

    B. Hashing

    C. Generators

    D. Integrity

28. **C** is correct. Generators can provide power to a data center if the power fails ensuring that the servers within the datacenter continue to operate.

A is incorrect. Encryption increases the confidentiality of data within the datacenter.

B and D are incorrect. Hashing verifies integrity.

Objective: 2.5 Compare and contrast aspects of business continuity

29. Your building is researching the costs and functionality of fire alarm systems for a new building. What capability should the system include to prevent a fire from spreading?

    A. Integration with a temperature control system

    B. Integration with a CCTV

    C. Integration with an HVAC system

    D. Integration with proximity card readers

29. **C** is correct. A fire alarm system should be integrated with an HVAC system so that the HVAC system can control airflow when a fire is detected.

A is incorrect. An HVAC includes a thermostat to regulate temperature, but this is for normal operation unrelated to fire prevention.

B is incorrect. A CCTV can detect if an unauthorized entry occurred and provide reliable proof of the entry, but is not related to fire.

D is incorrect. Proximity cards can help prevent unauthorized personnel from entering a secure datacenter.

Objective: 2.6 Explain the impact and proper use of environmental controls

30. An organization designed their datacenter with hot and cold aisles. Of the following choices, what is not a valid purpose of hot and cold aisles?

    A. Regulate cooling

    B. Increase availability

    C. Reduce cooling costs

    D. Fire suppression

30. **D** is correct. Hot and cold aisles do not suppress fires.

A is incorrect. They regulate cooling in datacenters, reducing cooling costs.

B and C are incorrect. If the datacenter temperature is adequately controlled in a data center, it reduces outages due to overheating and increases availability.

Objective: 2.6 Explain the impact and proper use of environmental controls

31. Your organization hosts several bays of servers within a server room. What environmental control within the datacenter requires a thermostat?

> A. Temperature control
>
> B. Hot and cold aisles
>
> C. Humidity control
>
> D. Generators

31. **A** is correct. A thermostat ensures that the temperature within a server room or datacenter is controlled and regulated.

B is incorrect. Hot and cold aisles are a design principle used to regulate cooling in datacenters, reducing cooling costs.

C is incorrect. A thermostat can't regulate humidity, though a moisture control system is often used to maintain humidity.

D is incorrect. Generators are used as an alternative power source.

Objective: 2.6 Explain the impact and proper use of environmental controls

32. An organization hosts several bays of servers used to support a large online ecommerce business. They want to ensure that customer data hosted within the datacenter is protected and they implement several access controls including an HVAC system. What does this the HVAC system help protect?

> A. Access
>
> B. Availability
>
> C. Confidentiality
>
> D. Integrity

32. **B** is correct. A Heating, Ventilation, and Air Conditioning (HVAC) system can increase availability by ensuring that equipment doesn't fail due to overheating.

A is incorrect. An HVAC system doesn't contribute to access control.

C is incorrect. Confidentiality ensures that data is only viewable by authorized users and can be ensured with access controls or encryption.

D is incorrect. Integrity provides assurances that data has not been modified, tampered with, or corrupted.

Objective: 2.6 Explain the impact and proper use of environmental controls

33. Of the following choices, what is the best choice to help prevent someone from capturing network traffic?

    A. EMI shielding

    B. Use hubs instead of switches

    C. Ensure that SNMP traps are set

    D. Hot and cold aisles

33. **A** is correct. Electromagnetic interference (EMI) shielding can protect a signal from interference from outside sources, and it can help prevent an attacker from capturing network traffic without tapping into the cable.

B is incorrect. Switches are an improvement over hubs (not hubs instead of switches) when trying to protect against an attacker capturing network traffic.

C is incorrect. SNMP traps can provide notifications from SNMP agents to SNMP servers related to the monitoring of network devices, but do not limit data captures.

D is incorrect. Hot and cold aisles regulate airflow in datacenters.

Objective: 2.6 Explain the impact and proper use of environmental controls

34. Which of the following provides fault tolerance through disk mirroring?

    A. RAID-0

    B. RAID-1

    C. RAID-5

    D. Clustering

34. **B** is correct. RAID-1 uses two disks and is also known as disk mirroring.

A is incorrect. RAID-0 does not provide fault tolerance.

C is incorrect. RAID-5 uses three or more disks and is known as striping with parity.

D is incorrect. Clustering provides fault tolerance to servers, not disks.

Objective: 2.7 Execute disaster recovery plans and procedures

35. An administrator is improving the availability of a server and needs to ensure that a hard drive failure does not result in the failure of the server. What will support this goal? (Choose all that apply.)

    A. Hardware RAID-0

    B. Hardware RAID-1

C. Software RAID-1

D. Software RAID-5

35. **B, C,** and **D** are correct. RAID-1 and RAID-5 provide fault tolerance for disk subsystems and will increase availability. While hardware RAID is quicker than software RAID, both will provide fault tolerance.

A is incorrect. RAID-0 increases performance but it does not provide fault tolerance.

Objective: 2.7 Execute disaster recovery plans and procedures

36. What can remove a server as a single point of failure?

A. RAID-1

B. Mirroring

C. Clustering

D. UPS

36. **C** is correct. Failover clustering removes a server as a single point of failure by including additional servers that can take over the service if the server fails.

A and B are incorrect. RAID-1 (also called mirroring) removes a drive (not a server) as a single point of failure.

D is incorrect. UPS provides fault tolerance for power failures.

Objective: 2.7 Execute disaster recovery plans and procedures

37. Several servers in your server room are connected to an UPS. What does this provide?

    A. Continuity of operations

    B. Disaster recovery

    C. Fault tolerance

    D. Long term power if commercial power fails

37. **C** is correct. An uninterrupted power supply (UPS) provides fault tolerance and allows the servers to continue to operate for a short period even if commercial power fails.

A is incorrect. Continuity of operations (COOP) focuses on restoring critical functions at an alternate site such as a hot, warm, or cold site.

B is incorrect. Disaster recovery restores systems after a recovery is not the same as fault tolerance.

D is incorrect. Generators (not UPS) provide long-term power if commercial power fails.

Objective: 2.7 Execute disaster recovery plans and procedures

38. What helps ensure availability in the event of an extended power outage?

    A. UPS

    B. Failover clusters

    C. RAID

    D. Generators

38. **D** is correct. Generators provide long-term power if commercial power fails.

A is incorrect. An uninterrupted power supply (UPS) provides fault tolerance for a short period.

B and C are incorrect. RAID increases availability for disk systems and failover clusters remove servers as a single point of failure, but neither will help in an extended power outage.

Objective: 2.7 Execute disaster recovery plans and procedures

39. You need to implement a backup strategy that allows the fastest recovery of data. What provides the best solution?

    A. A full backup daily

    B. A full/differential strategy

    C. A full/incremental strategy

    D. A differential/incremental strategy

39. **A** is correct. The fastest strategy is a full backup every day of the week because a failure only requires restoring a single tape.

B is incorrect. A full/differential strategy will reduce the time required to do backups after the full and would require only two tapes to restore.

C is incorrect. A full/incremental strategy minimizes the time required to do backups, but usually requires restoring more tapes resulting in a longer recovery time.

D is incorrect. All backup strategies must include a full so a differential/incremental strategy will not work.

Objective: 2.7 Execute disaster recovery plans and procedures

40. An organization regularly performs backups of critical systems. Where should they keep a copy of the backups for retention?

    A. Off-site

    B. With the backed up systems

    C. On a mirrored drive of the backed up system

    D. On a cluster

40. **A** is correct. A copy of backups should be kept in an off-site location for retention purposes.

B and C are incorrect. If the backups are kept with the backed up systems or on system drives, they can be destroyed if the system is destroyed such as in a fire.

D is incorrect. A cluster provides fault tolerance for a server but the servers are commonly located in the same place.

Objective: 2.7 Execute disaster recovery plans and procedures

41. An organization wants to verify that a tape backup can be restored in its entirety. What should they do?

    A. Perform test restores of random files on the backup

    B. Perform test restores of the full backup

    C. Copy the backup to the hot site

    D. Copy the backup to the cold site

41. **B** is correct. The only way to verify the entire tape can be restored is to restore the entire backup.

A is incorrect. Randomly restoring an individual file does not verify the entire backup tape.

C is incorrect. While an organization may store an off-site backup of tapes at a hot site, this won't verify the tape.

D is incorrect. Cold sites would not have any systems or data so backups would not be copied there.

Objective: 2.7 Execute disaster recovery plans and procedures

42. A business impact analysis (BIA) determined that a critical business function has a Recovery Time Objective (RTO) of an hour. What site will meet this objective?

    A. Hot site

    B. Cold site

    C. Warm site

    D. RTO site

42. **A** is correct. A hot site includes all the elements to bring a critical function operational the quickest, and will meet the RTO objective of ensuring a function is restored within an hour.

B is incorrect. A cold site takes the longest to restore.

C is incorrect. Because the RPO is one hour (60 minutes), the site must be operational in 59 minutes or less and a warm site will take longer than this to become operational.

D is incorrect. The Recovery Time Objective (RTO) is related to the BIA but there is no such thing as an RTO site.

Objective: 2.7 Execute disaster recovery plans and procedures

43. Which of the following continuity of operations solutions is the most expensive?

    A. Hot site

    B. Cold site

    C. Warm site

    D. Clustered site

43. **A** is correct. Hot sites are the most expensive.

B is incorrect. Cold sites are the least expensive.

C is incorrect. Warm sites are less expensive than a hot site.

D is incorrect. There is no such thing as a clustered site.

Objective: 2.7 Execute disaster recovery plans and procedures

44. An organization is considering an alternate location as part of their business continuity plan. They want to identify a solution that provides a balance between cost and recovery time. What will they choose?

    A. Hot site

    B. Cold site

    C. Warm site

    D. Mirrored site

44. **C** is correct. A warm site is a cross between a hot site and a cold site.

A is incorrect. A hot site which has everything needed for operations and is the most expensive.

B is incorrect. A cold site only has power and connectivity and takes the longest to recover.

D is incorrect. A mirrored site is identical to the primary location and provides 100 percent availability.

Objective: 2.7 Execute disaster recovery plans and procedures

45. Of the following choices, what is needed in a cold site used for continuity of operations?

    A. Power and connectivity

    B. All required equipment

    C. All required equipment with up-to-date patches

    D. All required equipment with up-to-date patches and data

45. **A** is correct. A cold site will have power and connectivity but little else.

B, C, and D are incorrect. A hot site will have all the required equipment with up-to-date patches, up-to-date data, and personnel.

Objective: 2.7 Execute disaster recovery plans and procedures

46. An organization is performing a disaster recovery exercise. Of the following choices, what is likely to be included?

    A. Test server restoration

    B. Picking a hot, warm, or cold site

    C. Creation of BIA

    D. Determination of the failsafe state

46. **A** is correct. A simple disaster recovery exercise rebuilds a server to validate the steps.

B is incorrect. The disaster recovery plan (DRP) documents the alternate site choice, but an exercise doesn't pick this location.

C is incorrect. The business impact analysis (BIA) identifies the Recovery Point Objectives (RPOs) and Recovery Time Objectives (RTOs) used in the DRP but it would be created before testing the plan.

D is incorrect. The failure state is dependent on availability and security requirements and not determined during a disaster recovery exercise.

Objective: 2.7 Execute disaster recovery plans and procedures

47. An organization implemented a disaster recovery plan in response to a hurricane. What is the last step in the disaster recovery process?

    A. Activation

    B. Recover systems

    C. Test systems

    D. Review

47. **D** is correct. The final phase of a disaster recovery includes a review to identify lessons learned and possibly update the disaster recovery plan (DRP).

A, B, and C are incorrect. In general, the order of the phases is activation, implement contingencies, recovery, testing (including comparing them against baselines), and review.

Objective: 2.7 Execute disaster recovery plans and procedures

48. An administrator used a disaster recovery plan to rebuild a critical server after an attack. Of the following choices, how can the administrator verify the system's functionality?

    A. Perform a review of the recovery process

    B. Install approved changes

    C. Compare the system's performance against a performance baseline

    D. Removed antivirus software

48. **C** is correct. The functionality can be verified by comparing the system's performance against a performance baseline.

A is incorrect. The last phase of disaster recovery is a review, but this won't verify the system's functionality.

B is incorrect. The recovery should include installing approved changes and updates, but this doesn't verify functionality.

D is incorrect. Antivirus software should not be removed.

Objective: 2.7 Execute disaster recovery plans and procedures

49. A critical system failed. Of the following choices, what would an organization implement to restore it?

    A. BIA

    B. DRP

    C. COOP

    D. RAID

49. **B** is correct. An organization would implement a disaster recovery plan (DRP) to restore a critical system after a disruption or failure.

A is incorrect. A business impact analysis (BIA) identifies the Recovery Point Objectives (RPOs) and Recovery Time Objectives (RTOs).

C is incorrect. A continuity of operations (COOP) site is an alternate site such as a hot, warm, or cold site.

D is incorrect. Redundant array of independent disks (RAID) is used to increase availability of disk subsystems.

Objective: 2.7 Execute disaster recovery plans and procedures

50. A database administrator is tasked with increasing the retail prices of all products in a database by 10 percent. The administrator writes a script performing a bulk update of the database and executes it. However, all retail prices are doubled (increased by 100 percent instead of 10 percent). What has been lost?

    A. Confidentiality

    B. Integrity

    C. Hashing

    D. Authentication

50. **B** is correct. The database has lost integrity through an unintended change.

A is incorrect. Loss of confidentiality indicates that unauthorized users have accessed the database.

C is incorrect. Hashing can be used to verify integrity in some situations (though not in this scenario), but hashing would not be compromised.

D is incorrect. Authentication provides proof that users are who they claim to be.

Objective: 2.8 Exemplify the concepts of confidentiality, integrity and availability (CIA)

51. You want to ensure that data has not been changed between the time when it was sent and when it arrived at its destination. What provides this assurance?

    A. Confidentiality

    B. Integrity

    C. Availability

    D. Authentication

51. B is correct. Integrity provides assurances that data has not been modified and is enforced with hashing.

A is incorrect. Confidentiality prevents unauthorized disclosure and is enforced with access controls and encryption.

C is incorrect. Availability ensures systems are up and operational when needed and uses fault tolerance and redundancy methods.

D is incorrect. Authentication provides proof that users are who they claim to be.

Objective: 2.8 Exemplify the concepts of confidentiality, integrity and availability (CIA)

52. You are planning to host a free online forum for users to share IT security related information with each other. Any user can anonymously view data. They can post messages after logging in but you do not want them to be able modify other user's posts. What levels of confidentiality, integrity, and availability should you seek?

    A. Low confidentiality, low integrity, and low availability

    B. Medium confidentiality, low integrity, and high availability

    C. High confidentiality, low integrity, and low availability

    D. Low confidentiality, medium integrity, and medium availability

52. **D** is correct. Data can be viewed anonymously so low confidentiality is acceptable.

A, B, and C are incorrect. You do not want users to modify other user's posts so integrity is medium.

A and C are incorrect. The site is free but you do want users to be able to access it when needed so availability is medium.

Objective: 2.8 Exemplify the concepts of confidentiality, integrity and availability (CIA)

53. You want to ensure that data is only viewable by authorized users. What security principle are you trying to enforce?

    A. Confidentiality

    B. Integrity

    C. Availability

    D. Authentication

53. **A** is correct. Confidentiality ensures that data is only viewable by authorized users and can be ensured with access controls and encryption.

B is incorrect. Integrity is enforced with hashing.

C is incorrect. Availability can be ensured with power and cooling systems, and various fault tolerance and redundancy techniques.

D is incorrect. Authentication proves a person's identity and is a first step in access control, but by itself it does not provide confidentiality.

Objective: 2.8 Exemplify the concepts of confidentiality, integrity and availability (CIA)

Chapter 3 Threats and Vulnerabilities

Threats and Vulnerabilities topics are **21 percent** of the CompTIA Security+ exam. The objectives in this domain are:

3.1 Analyze and differentiate among types of malware
- Adware
- Virus
- Worms
- Spyware
- Trojan
- Rootkits
- Backdoors
- Logic bomb
- Botnets

3.2 Analyze and differentiate among types of attacks
- Man-in-the-middle
- DDoS
- DoS
- Replay
- Smurf attack
- Spoofing
- Spam
- Phishing
- Spim
- Vishing
- Spear phishing
- Xmas attack
- Pharming

- Privilege escalation
- Malicious insider threat
- DNS poisoning and ARP poisoning
- Transitive access
- Client-side attacks

3.3 Analyze and differentiate among types of social engineering attacks
- Shoulder surfing
- Dumpster diving
- Tailgating
- Impersonation
- Hoaxes
- Whaling
- Vishing

3.4 Analyze and differentiate among types of wireless attacks
- Rogue access points
- Interference
- Evil twin
- War driving
- Bluejacking
- Bluesnarfing
- War chalking
- IV attack
- Packet sniffing

3.5 Analyze and differentiate among types of application attacks
- Cross-site scripting
- SQL injection
- LDAP injection
- XML injection
- Directory traversal/command injection
- Buffer overflow

- Zero day
- Cookies and attachments
- Malicious add-ons
- Session hijacking
- Header manipulation

3.6 Analyze and differentiate among types of mitigation and deterrent techniques
- Manual bypassing of electronic controls
  - Failsafe/secure vs. failopen
- Monitoring system logs
  - Event logs
  - Audit logs
  - Security logs
  - Access logs
- Physical security
  - Hardware locks
  - Mantraps
  - Video surveillance
  - Fencing
  - Proximity readers
  - Access list
- Hardening
  - Disabling unnecessary services
  - Protecting management interfaces and applications
  - Password protection
  - Disabling unnecessary accounts
- Port security
  - MAC limiting and filtering
  - 802.1x
  - Disabling unused ports
- Security posture
  - Initial baseline configuration
  - Continuous security monitoring
  - Remediation
- Reporting

- o Alarms
- o Alerts
- o Trends
- Detection controls vs. prevention controls
  - o IDS vs. IPS
  - o Camera vs. guard

3.7 Implement assessment tools and techniques to discover security threats and vulnerabilities
- Vulnerability scanning and interpret results
- Tools
  - o Protocol analyzer
  - o Sniffer
  - o Vulnerability scanner
  - o Honeypots
  - o Honeynets
  - o Port scanner
- Risk calculations
  - o Threat vs. likelihood
- Assessment types
  - o Risk
  - o Threat
  - o Vulnerability
- Assessment technique
  - o Baseline reporting
  - o Code review
  - o Determine attack surface
  - o Architecture
  - o Design reviews

3.8 Within the realm of vulnerability assessments, explain the proper use of penetration testing versus vulnerability scanning
- Penetration testing
  - o Verify a threat exists
  - o Bypass security controls
  - o Actively test security controls
  - o Exploiting vulnerabilities

- Vulnerability scanning
    - Passively testing security controls
    - Identify vulnerability
    - Identify lack of security controls
    - Identify common misconfiguration
- Black box
- White box
- Gray box

The CompTIA Security+: Get Certified Get Ahead SY0-301 Study Guide (ISBN 1463762364) discusses these topics in much more depth. Sec-plus.com has more details on the availability of this book.

√ **Get Certified**
  √ **Get Ahead**

Practice Test Questions for Threats and Vulnerabilities Domain

1. What is the difference between a worm and a virus?

    A. A worm is self-replicating but a virus isn't self-replicating.

    B. A virus is self-replicating but a worm isn't self-replicating.

    C. A virus runs in response to an event such as a date, but a worm runs on its own schedule.

    D. A worm runs in response to an event such as a date, but a virus runs on its own schedule.

2. After downloading pirated software, a user notices the computer is running very slowly and antivirus software is detecting malware. What likely happened?

    A. The user installed a Trojan.

    B. The user installed a worm.

    C. The user installed a logic bomb.

    D. The user installed a botnet.

3. What type of malware do users inadvertently install with USB thumb drives?

    A. Spam

    B. Trojans

    C. Buffer overflow

    D. Logic bomb

4. At 9 a.m. on January 31, an administrator starts receiving alerts from monitoring systems indicating problems with servers in the datacenter. He discovers that all servers are unreachable. Of the following choices, what is the most likely cause?

    A. Logic bomb

    B. XSRF attack

    C. Buffer overflow

    D. Rootkit

5. An employee has added malicious code into the company's personnel system. The code verifies the employment status of the employee once a month. If the check shows the person is no longer an active employee, it launches attacks on internal servers. What type of code is this?

    A. Botnet

    B. Logic bomb

    C. Trojan

    D. Adware

6. A process running on a system has system level access to the operating system kernel. Investigation shows that it has modified system files. What best describes this behavior?

    A. Rootkit

    B. Worm

    C. Cross-site scripting

    D. Adware

7. Where would a security specialist look for a hooked process?

    A. Rootkit

    B. Disk

    C. RAM

    D. Firewall log

8. A file integrity checker on a database server detected several modified system files. What could cause this?

    A. Spam

    B. Buffer overflow

    C. Logic bomb

    D. Rootkit

9. A user's system has spyware installed. What is the most likely result?

    A. Loss of root level access

    B. Loss of confidentiality

    C. Loss of integrity

    D. Loss of anonymity on the Internet

10. A user browsing the Internet notices erratic behavior right before the user's system crashes. After rebooting, the system is slow and the user detects hundreds of outbound connections. What likely occurred?

    A. The system has become a botnet.

    B. The system is hosting a botnet.

    C. The system is spamming other users.

    D. The system has joined a botnet.

11. A computer is regularly communicating with an unknown IRC server and sending traffic without user interaction. What is likely causing this?

    A. Buffer overflow

    B. Cross-site scripting

    C. Botnet

    D. Rootkit

12. Of the following choices, what uses a command and control server?

    A. DoS attacks

    B. Trojans

    C. Man-in-the -middle attacks

    D. Botnet

13. An attacker wants to obtain bank account information from a user. Which of the following methods do attackers use?

    A. Tailgating

    B. Fuzzing

    C. Password masking

    D. Phishing

14. Of the following choices, what best represents an attack against specific employees of a company?

    A. Phishing

    B. Vishing

    C. Spim

    D. Spear phishing

15. Attackers sent a targeted email attack to the President of a company. What best describes this attack?

    A. Phishing

    B. Spam

    C. Whaling

    D. Botnet

16. Bob reported receiving a message from his bank prompting him to call back about a credit card. When he called back, an automated recording prompted him to provide personal information to verify his identity and then provide details about his bank and credit card accounts. What type of attack is this?

    A. Phishing

    B. Whaling

    C. Vishing

    D. VoIP

17. An attacker enters a string of data in a web application's input form and crashes it. What type of attack is this?

    A. DoS

    B. DDoS

    C. Man-in-the-middle

    D. Header manipulation

18. Of the following choices, what type of attack can intercept traffic and insert malicious code into a network conversation?

    A. Spim

    B. Xmas attack

    C. LDAP injection

    D. Man-in-the-middle

19. An attacker is sending false hardware address updates to a system causing the system to redirect traffic to an attacker. What type of attack is this?

    A. IRC

    B. ARP poisoning

    C. Xmas attack

    D. DNS poisoning

20. What can mitigate ARP poisoning attacks in a network?

    A. Disable unused ports on a switch

    B. Man-in-the-middle

    C. DMZ

    D. VLAN segregation

21. While surfing the Internet, a user sees a message indicating a malware infection and offering free antivirus software. The user downloads the free antivirus software but realizes it infected this system. Which of the following choices best explains what happened to the user?

    A. Social engineering

B. Trojan

C. Vishing

D. Spim

22. An organization regularly shreds paper instead of throwing it away. What are they trying to prevent?

    A. Losses due to dumpster diving

    B. Losses due to data classification

    C. Losses due to data classification labeling

    D. Losses due to P2P

23. A person is trying to gain unauthorized information through casual observation. What type of attack is this?

    A. Tailgating

    B. Whaling

    C. Dumpster diving

    D. Shoulder surfing

24. A web application developer is suggesting using password masking in the application. What is the developer trying to prevent?

    A. Buffer overflow attacks

    B. Shoulder surfing

    C. SQL injection

    D. Cross-site scripting

25. Which one of the following secure protocols did WEP implement incorrectly allowing attackers to crack it?

A. SSL

B. RC4

C. CCMP

D. AES

26. While troubleshooting a problem with a WAP in your organization, you discover a rogue access point with the same SSID as the organization's WAP. What is this second access point?

    A. IDS

    B. War chalking

    C. Evil twin

    D. Packet sniffer

27. You want to identify the physical location of a rogue access point you discovered in the footprint of your company. What would you use?

    A. Bluesnarfing

    B. Bluejacking

    C. War chalking

    D. War driving

28. You are hosting a wireless hotspot and you want to segment each wireless user from each other. What should you use?

    A. Personal mode

    B. Enterprise mode

    C. Isolation mode

    D. WEP

29. Which of the following best describes bluejacking?

    A. Bluejacking involves accessing data on a phone.

    B. Bluejacking involves checking a WAPs antenna placement, power levels, and encryption techniques.

    C. Bluejacking involves sending unsolicited messages to a phone.

    D. Bluejacking involves a rogue access point with the same SSID as your production WAP.

30. Your organization wants to reduce threats from zero day vulnerabilities. Of the following choices, what provides the best solution?

    A. Opening ports on a server's firewall

    B. Disabling unnecessary services

    C. Keep systems up-to-date with current patches

    D. Keep systems up-to-date with current service packs

31. What can a header manipulation attack modify?

    A. Flags

    B. Buffers

    C. Databases

    D. Signature definitions

32. An IDS detected a NOOP sled. What kind of attack does this indicate?

    A. Input validation

    B. SQL injection

C. Cross-site scripting

D. Buffer overflow

33. A web-based application expects a user to enter eight characters into a text box. However, the application allows a user to copy more than eight characters into the text box. What is a potential vulnerability for this application?

    A. Input validation

    B. Buffer overflow

    C. SYN flood

    D. Flood guard

34. While analyzing an application log, you discover several entries where a user has entered the following command into a web-based form: ../etc/passwd. What does this indicate?

    A. Fuzzing

    B. Kiting

    C. Command injection attack

    D. DoS

35. What will protect against a SYN attack?

    A. Input validation

    B. Error handling

    C. Flood guard

    D. Cross-site scripting

36. What can an administrator use to detect a DDoS attack?

    A. Privilege escalation

    B. Performance baseline

    C. Web form sanitization

    D. Antivirus software

37. You want to check a log to determine when a user logged on and off of a system. What log would you check?

    A. System

    B. Application

    C. Firewall

    D. Security

38. Which of the following is a preventative control that can prevent outages due to ad-hoc configuration errors?

    A. Least privilege

    B. A periodic review of user rights

    C. Change management plan

    D. Security audit

39. Which of the following is a preventative control?

    A. Least privilege

    B. Security audit

    C. Security guard

    D. Periodic review of user rights

40. Your organization regularly performs routine security audits to assess the security posture. What type of control is this?

    A. Corrective

    B. Technical

    C. Detective

    D. Preventative

41. Of the following choices, what is a detective security control?

    A. Change management

    B. HVAC

    C. CCTV

    D. User training

42. What is the purpose of a cipher lock system?

    A. Control door access with a keypad

    B. Control door access with a proximity card

    C. Control access to a laptop with biometrics

    D. Control access to laptop with a smart card.

43. What can you use to electronically unlock a door for specific users?

    A. Token

    B. Proximity card

    C. Physical key

    D. Certificate

44. An organization wants to prevent unauthorized personnel from entering a secure workspace. Of the following choices, what can be used? (Choose two).

    A. Security guard

    B. Piggybacking

    C. CCTV

    D. Proximity cards

45. A company hosts a datacenter with highly sensitive data. Of the following choices, what can provide the best type of physical security to prevent unauthorized entry?

    A. Proximity card

    B. CCTV

    C. ID badges

    D. Mantrap

46. You are evaluating the security and availability of a system. Security is more important than availability in the system. If it fails, what state should it fail in?

    A. It should fail open

    B. It should fail closed

    C. It should shut down

    D. It should be rebooted

47. Two employees have entered a secure datacenter. However, only one employee provided credentials. How did the other employee gain entry?

    A. Mantrap

    B. HVAC

    C. Vishing

    D. Tailgating

48. You have recently added a server to your network that will host data used and updated by employees. You want to monitor security events on the system. Of the following, what is the most important security event to monitor?

    A. Data modifications

    B. TCP connections

    C. UDP connections

    D. Account logon attempts

49. What is included in a risk assessment? (Choose three.)

    A. Threats

    B. Vulnerabilities

    C. Asset values

    D. Recommendations to eliminate risk

50. Which of the following statements are true regarding risk assessments? (Choose two.)

    A. A quantitative risk assessment uses hard numbers.

    B. A qualitative risk assessment uses on hard numbers.

C. A qualitative risk assessment uses a subjective ranking.

D. A quantitative risk assessment uses a subjective ranking.

51. A security professional is performing a qualitative risk analysis. Of the following choices, what will most likely to be used in the assessment?

A. Cost

B. Judgment

C. ALE

D. Hard numbers

52. An organization recently completed a risk assessment. Who should be granted access to the report?

A. All employees

B. Security professionals only

C. Executive management only

D. Security professionals and executive management

53. A security administrator is performing a vulnerability assessment. Which of the following actions would be included?

A. Implement a password policy

B. Delete unused accounts

C. Organize data based on severity and asset value

D. Remove system rights for users that don't need them

54. An organization has released an application. Of the following choices, what is the most thorough way to discover vulnerabilities with the application?

    A. Fuzzing

    B. OVAL comparison

    C. Rainbow table

    D. Code review

55. Which of the following tools can perform a port scan? (Choose all that apply.)

    A. Nmap

    B. Netcat

    C. Wireshark

    D. Netstat

56. What can you use to examine IP headers in a data packet?

    A. Protocol analyzer

    B. Port scanner

    C. Vulnerability scanner

    D. Penetration tester

57. What can you use to examine text transmitted over a network by an application?

    A. Honeypot

    B. Honeynet

    C. Protocol analyzer

    D. Vulnerability scanner

58. An administrator suspects that a computer is sending out large amounts of sensitive data to an external system. What tool can the administrator use to verify this?

    A. Rainbow table

    B. Protocol analyzer

    C. Password cracker

    D. Port scanner

59. An administrator suspects that a web application is sending database credentials across the network in clear text. What can the administrator use to verify this?

    A. SQL injection

    B. Protocol analyzer

    C. A network-based DLP

    D. Password cracker

60. Sally used WinZip to create an archive of several sensitive documents on an upcoming merger and she password-protected the archive file. Of the following choices, what is the best way to test the security of the archive file?

    A. Rainbow table

    B. Vulnerability scanner

    C. Password cracker

    D. Sniffer

61. Of the following choices, what can you use to divert malicious attacks on your network away from valuable resources to relatively worthless resources?

A. IDS

B. Proxy server

C. Web application firewall

D. Honeypot

62. An organization develops its own software. Of the following choices what is a security practice that should be included in the process?

    A. Check vendor documentation

    B. SDLC Waterfall model

    C. Code review

    D. Enabling command injection

63. You are trying to determine what systems on your network are most susceptible to an attack. What tool would you use?

    A. Port scanner

    B. SQL injection

    C. Header manipulation

    D. Vulnerability scanner

64. A security administrator used a tool to discover security issues, but did not exploit them. What best describes this action?

    A. Penetration test

    B. Vulnerability scan

    C. Protocol analysis

    D. Port scan

65. An administrator needs to test the security of a network without affecting normal operations. What can the administrator use?

  A. Internal penetration test

  B. External penetration test

  C. Vulnerability scanner

  D. Protocol analyzer

66. A security administrator wants to scan the network for a wide range of potential security and configuration issues. What tool provides this service?

  A. Fuzzer

  B. Protocol analyzer

  C. Port scanner

  D. Vulnerability scanner

67. A security professional is performing a penetration test on a system. Of the following choices, what identifies the best description of what this will accomplish?

  A. Passively detect vulnerabilities

  B. Actively assess security controls

  C. Identify lack of security controls

  D. Identify common misconfiguration

68. An organization is hiring a security firm to perform vulnerability testing. What should they define before the testing?

  A. Rules of engagement

  B. Information given to the black box testers

C. Vulnerabilities

D. Existing security controls

69. An organization wants to test how well employees can respond to a compromised system. Of the following choices, what identifies the best choice to test the response?

A. Vulnerability scan

B. White hat test

C. Black hat test

D. Penetration test

70. Testers have access to product documentation and source code for an application that they are using in a vulnerability test. What type of test is this?

A. Black box

B. White box

C. Black hat

D. White hat

71. A tester is fuzzing an application. What is another name for this?

A. Black box testing

B. White box testing

C. Gray box testing

D. Black hat testing

Practice Test Questions with Answers for Threats and Vulnerabilities Domain

1. What is the difference between a worm and a virus?

    A. A worm is self-replicating but a virus isn't self-replicating.

    B. A virus is self-replicating but a worm isn't self-replicating.

    C. A virus runs in response to an event such as a date, but a worm runs on its own schedule.

    D. A worm runs in response to an event such as a date, but a virus runs on its own schedule.

1. **A** is correct. A worm is self-replicating.

B is incorrect. Viruses are not self-replicating but require user interaction to run.

C and D are incorrect. A logic bomb runs in response to an event such as a date, but worms and viruses do not run in response to events.

Objective: 3.1 Analyze and differentiate among types of malware

2. After downloading pirated software, a user notices the computer is running very slowly and antivirus software is detecting malware. What likely happened?

    A. The user installed a Trojan.

    B. The user installed a worm.

    C. The user installed a logic bomb.

    D. The user installed a botnet.

2. **A** is correct. A Trojan appears to be something useful but instead includes something malicious and in this case, the pirated software included malware.

B is incorrect. Worms are self-replicating.

C is incorrect. Logic bombs execute in response to an event such as time.

D is incorrect. A user may join a botnet such as after visiting a malicious website, but a user does not install a botnet.

Objective: 3.1 Analyze and differentiate among types of malware

3. What type of malware do users inadvertently install with USB thumb drives?

    A. Spam

    B. Trojans

    C. Buffer overflow

    D. Logic bomb

3. **B** is correct. Users can unknowingly transfer and install Trojan horse malware onto their systems with USB thumb drives.

A is incorrect. Spam is unwanted email filtered with antispam software.

C is incorrect. A buffer overflow occurs when a system receives unexpected data or more data than program can handle.

D is incorrect. A logic bomb is a program or code snippet that executes in response to an event, such as a specific time or date.

Objective: 3.1 Analyze and differentiate among types of malware

4. At 9 a.m. on January 31, an administrator starts receiving alerts from monitoring systems indicating problems with servers in the datacenter. He discovers that all servers are unreachable. Of the following choices, what is the most likely cause?

    A. Logic bomb

    B. XSRF attack

    C. Buffer overflow

    D. Rootkit

4. **A** is correct. A logic bomb is a program or code snippet that executes in response to an event such as a specific time or date and since all the servers are affected at the same time, this is the most likely cause.

B is incorrect. A cross-site request forgery (XSRF) attack occurs when an attacker tricks a user into performing an action on a web site.

C is incorrect. A buffer overflow attack occurs when an attacker sends more data to a single system than it can handle and overwrites memory locations, and would not affect all servers at the same time.

D is incorrect. A rootkit provide attackers with system or kernel access on a single system and can modify file system operations for a single system.

Objective: 3.1 Analyze and differentiate among types of malware

5. An employee has added malicious code into the company's personnel system. The code verifies the employment status of the employee once a month. If the check shows the person is no longer an active employee, it launches attacks on internal servers. What type of code is this?

    A. Botnet

    B. Logic bomb

    C. Trojan

    D. Adware

5. **B** is correct. A logic bomb is a program or code snippet that executes in response to an event and can execute after checking for a condition.

A is incorrect. A botnet is group of computers controlled through command and control software, and commonly launches DDoS attacks.

C is incorrect. A Trojan appears to be something useful but instead includes something malicious, but the code in this question is strictly malicious.

D is incorrect. Adware may open and close windows with advertisements and pop-up blockers can block it.

Objective: 3.1 Analyze and differentiate among types of malware

6. A process running on a system has system level access to the operating system kernel. Investigation shows that it has modified system files. What best describes this behavior?

    A. Rootkit

B. Worm

C. Cross-site scripting

D. Adware

6. A is correct. Rootkits provide attackers with system level (or kernel) access and can modify file system operations.

B is incorrect. A worm is self-replicating malware but wouldn't typically have system level access.

C is incorrect. Cross-site scripting allows an attacker to inject malicious code into a web site's HTML pages.

D is incorrect. Adware may open and close windows with advertisements, but wouldn't modify administrative access.

Objective: 3.1 Analyze and differentiate among types of malware

7. Where would a security specialist look for a hooked process?

A. Rootkit

B. Disk

C. RAM

D. Firewall log

7. **C** is correct. Processes (including hooked processes) are stored and run from random access memory (RAM) so experts look in RAM for hooked processes.

A is incorrect. A rootkit commonly uses a hooked process, but examining files in the rootkit would not identify a hooked process.

B is incorrect. Rootkit files would be stored on the drive but not hooked processes.

D is incorrect. A firewall log can record firewall activity but it wouldn't include information on hooked processes.

Objective: 3.1 Analyze and differentiate among types of malware

8. A file integrity checker on a database server detected several modified system files. What could cause this?

    A. Spam

    B. Buffer overflow

    C. Logic bomb

    D. Rootkit

8. **D** is correct. Rootkits have system level (or kernel) access and can modify system files (detectable with host-based intrusion detection systems or antivirus software file integrity checkers).

A is incorrect. Spam is unwanted email and doesn't modify system files.

B is incorrect. A buffer overflow occurs when a vulnerable application receives unexpected data that it can't handle, but it isn't necessarily an attack.

C is incorrect. A logic bomb is a program or code snippet that executes in response to an event such as a specific time or date.

Objective: 3.1 Analyze and differentiate among types of malware

9. A user's system has spyware installed. What is the most likely result?

    A. Loss of root level access

    B. Loss of confidentiality

    C. Loss of integrity

    D. Loss of anonymity on the Internet

9. **B** is correct. Spyware collects user data and results in the loss of confidentiality.

A is incorrect. A rootkit may remove a user's root level access.

C is incorrect. Spyware rarely disables systems or modifies data so integrity is not lost, though spyware may slow a system down.

D is incorrect. There is no such thing as anonymity on the Internet, with or without spyware.

Objective: 3.1 Analyze and differentiate among types of malware

10. A user browsing the Internet notices erratic behavior right before the user's system crashes. After rebooting, the system is slow and the user detects hundreds of outbound connections. What likely occurred?

    A. The system has become a botnet.

    B. The system is hosting a botnet.

    C. The system is spamming other users.

    D. The system has joined a botnet.

10. **D** is correct. This describes a drive by download that downloads malware onto a user's system after visiting a web site, and joins it to a botnet (indicated by the hundreds of outbound connections).

A and B are incorrect. A botnet is composed of multiple systems, not a single system and criminals (known as bot herders) control the systems in the botnet.

C is incorrect. Botnets members can spam (and attack) others but the symptoms don't indicate that this what is happening.

Objective: 3.1 Analyze and differentiate among types of malware

11. A computer is regularly communicating with an unknown IRC server and sending traffic without user interaction. What is likely causing this?

    A. Buffer overflow

    B. Cross-site scripting

    C. Botnet

    D. Rootkit

11. **C** is correct. Botnets control computers in the botnet and can use Internet Relay Chat (IRC) messages.

A is incorrect. A buffer overflow occurs when a system receives unexpected data such as a string of NOOP instructions.

B is incorrect. Cross-site scripting allows an attacker to inject malicious code into a web site's HTML pages.

D is incorrect. Rootkits provide attackers with system level access and can modify file system operations, but don't use IRC.

Objective: 3.1 Analyze and differentiate among types of malware

12. Of the following choices, what uses a command and control server?

    A. DoS attacks

    B. Trojans

    C. Man-in-the -middle attacks

    D. Botnet

12. **D** is correct. Criminals control botnets through command and control software running on Internet servers.

A is incorrect. Botnets frequently launch DDoS attacks from each system, but not DoS attacks from a single system.

B is incorrect. A Trojan is malware that appears to be something useful but instead includes something malicious.

C is incorrect. A man-in-the-middle attack can intercept traffic and insert malicious code but it doesn't use a command and control server.

Objective: 3.1 Analyze and differentiate among types of malware

13. An attacker wants to obtain bank account information from a user. Which of the following methods do attackers use?

    A. Tailgating

    B. Fuzzing

    C. Password masking

    D. Phishing

13. **D** is correct. Phishing is the practice of sending email to users with the purpose of tricking them into revealing personal information (such as bank account information).

A is incorrect. Tailgating occurs when one user follows closely behind another user without using credentials and mantraps help prevent tailgating.

B is incorrect. Fuzzing, or fuzz testing, sends invalid, unexpected, or random data to a system to detect buffer overflow vulnerabilities.

C is incorrect. Password masking displays a special character, such as an asterisk (*), instead of the password to prevent shoulder surfing.

Objective: 3.2 Analyze and differentiate among types of attacks

14. Of the following choices, what best represents an attack against specific employees of a company?

    A. Phishing

    B. Vishing

    C. Spim

    D. Spear phishing

14. **D** is correct. A spear phishing attack targets a specific person or specific groups of people such as employees of a company.

A is incorrect. Phishing sends email to users with the purpose of tricking them into revealing personal information, such as bank account information, but it doesn't target specific employees of a company.

B is incorrect. Vishing is a form of phishing that uses recorded voice over the telephone.

C is incorrect. Spim is a form of spam using instant messaging (IM).

Objective: 3.2 Analyze and differentiate among types of attacks

15. Attackers sent a targeted email attack to the President of a company. What best describes this attack?

    A. Phishing

    B. Spam

    C. Whaling

    D. Botnet

15. **C** is correct. Whaling is a phishing attack that targets high-level executives.

A is incorrect. Phishing sends email to users with the purpose of tricking them into revealing personal information (such as bank account information), but it doesn't target users.

B is incorrect. Spam is unsolicited email and phishing and whaling attacks are sent as spam, but spam itself isn't a targeted attack.

D is incorrect. A botnet is a group of computers joined to a network and criminals control them with command and control servers.

Objective: 3.2 Analyze and differentiate among types of attacks

16. Bob reported receiving a message from his bank prompting him to call back about a credit card. When he called back, an automated recording prompted him to provide personal information to verify his identity and then provide details about his bank and credit card accounts. What type of attack is this?

    A. Phishing

    B. Whaling

    C. Vishing

    D. VoIP

16. **C** is correct. Vishing is a form of phishing that uses recorded voice over the telephone.

A is incorrect. Phishing sends email to users with the purpose of tricking them into revealing personal information (such as bank account information).

B is incorrect. Whaling is a phishing attack that targets high-level executives.

D is incorrect. Vishing attacks often use Voice over IP (VoIP) but VoIP isn't an attack.

Objective: 3.2 Analyze and differentiate among types of attacks

17. An attacker enters a string of data in a web application's input form and crashes it. What type of attack is this?

    A. DoS

    B. DDoS

    C. Man-in-the-middle

    D. Header manipulation

17. A is correct. The question describes a buffer overflow attack, which can be used as a denial-of-service (DoS) attack.

B is incorrect. A DDoS attack comes from multiple computers.

C is incorrect. A man in the middle attack can interrupt network traffic and insert malicious code into a session but it doesn't attack applications.

D is incorrect. A header manipulation manipulates flags and data in packets.

Objective: 3.2 Analyze and differentiate among types of attacks, 3.5 Analyze and differentiate among types of application attacks

18. Of the following choices, what type of attack can intercept traffic and insert malicious code into a network conversation?

    A. Spim

    B. Xmas attack

    C. LDAP injection

D. Man-in-the-middle

18. **D** is correct. A man-in-the-middle attack can intercept traffic and insert malicious code, but Kerberos helps prevent man-in-the-middle attacks with mutual authentication.

A is incorrect. Spim attacks send messages over instant messaging channels but can't intercept traffic.

B is incorrect. A Xmas attack is a port scan attack where an attacker attempts to detect the operating system of the scanned system.

C is incorrect. LDAP injection is an attack used against Active Directory based systems.

Objective: 3.2 Analyze and differentiate among types of attacks

19. An attacker is sending false hardware address updates to a system causing the system to redirect traffic to an attacker. What type of attack is this?

    A. IRC

    B. ARP poisoning

    C. Xmas attack

    D. DNS poisoning

19. **B** is correct. Hardware addresses are MAC addresses, and an ARP poisoning attack misleads computers or switches about the actual MAC address of a system and can redirect traffic.

A is incorrect. Botnets sometimes communicate via IRC channels but IRC channels don't send false updates to a switch.

C is incorrect. An Xmas attack is a port scan where an attacker attempts to detect the operating system of the scanned system.

D is incorrect. DNS poisoning attacks corrupt name resolution data used to resolve names to IP addresses.

Objective: 3.2 Analyze and differentiate among types of attacks

20. What can mitigate ARP poisoning attacks in a network?

    A. Disable unused ports on a switch

    B. Man-in-the-middle

    C. DMZ

    D. VLAN segregation

20. **D** is correct. Address Resolution Protocol (ARP) poisoning attacks modify the hardware addresses in ARP cache to redirect traffic, and virtual local area network (VLAN) segregation can limit the scope of these attacks.

A is incorrect. Disabling unused physical ports on a switch is a good security practice, but it doesn't prevent ARP poisoning attacks.

B is incorrect. A man-in-the middle attack can interrupt traffic, insert malicious code, and ARP poisoning is one way to launch a man-in-the middle attack.

C is incorrect. A DMZ provides access to services from Internet clients, while segmenting access to an internal network.

Objective: 3.2 Analyze and differentiate among types of attacks

21. While surfing the Internet, a user sees a message indicating a malware infection and offering free antivirus software. The user downloads the free antivirus software but realizes it infected this system. Which of the following choices best explains what happened to the user?

    A. Social engineering

    B. Trojan

    C. Vishing

    D. Spim

21. **A** is correct. The user was tricked by the web site using a sophisticated form of social engineering.

B is incorrect. The system, not the user, was infected with a Trojan commonly known as rogueware or scareware.

C is incorrect. Vishing is a form of phishing that uses recorded voice over the telephone.

D is incorrect. Spim is a form of spam using instant messaging (IM).

Objective: 3.3 Analyze and differentiate among types of social engineering attacks, 3.1 Analyze and differentiate among types of malware

22. An organization regularly shreds paper instead of throwing it away. What are they trying to prevent?

    A. Losses due to dumpster diving

    B. Losses due to data classification

    C. Losses due to data classification labeling

    D. Losses due to P2P

22. **A** is correct. Dumpster divers search through trash looking for information and shredding mitigates the threat.

B is incorrect. Data classification helps protect sensitive data by ensuring users understand the value of data.

C is incorrect. Data labeling ensures that users know what data they are handling and processing.

D is incorrect. Peer-to-peer (P2P) and file sharing applications cause data leakage, and port scanners can detect P2P applications.

Objective: 3.3 Analyze and differentiate among types of social engineering attacks

23. A person is trying to gain unauthorized information through casual observation. What type of attack is this?

    A. Tailgating

    B. Whaling

    C. Dumpster diving

    D. Shoulder surfing

23. **D** is correct. Shoulder surfing is an attempt to gain unauthorized information through casual observation such as looking over someone's shoulder and password masking helps mitigate the risk.

A is incorrect. Tailgating is the practice of one person following closely behind another without showing credentials and mantraps help prevent tailgating.

B is incorrect. Whaling is a phishing attack that targets high-level executives.

C is incorrect. Dumpster divers search through trash looking for information and shredding documents can mitigate their success.

Objective: 3.3 Analyze and differentiate among types of social engineering attacks

24. A web application developer is suggesting using password masking in the application. What is the developer trying to prevent?

    A. Buffer overflow attacks

    B. Shoulder surfing

    C. SQL injection

    D. Cross-site scripting

24. **B** is correct. Password masking displays a special character, such as an asterisk (*), instead of the password to prevent shoulder surfing.

A, C, and D are incorrect. Input validation checks input data and can help mitigate buffer overflow, SQL injection, and cross-site scripting attacks.

Objective: 3.3 Analyze and differentiate among types of social engineering attacks

25. Which one of the following secure protocols did WEP implement incorrectly allowing attackers to crack it?

    A. SSL

    B. RC4

    C. CCMP

    D. AES

25. **B** is correct. Wired Equivalent Privacy (WEP) implemented RC4 with small initialization vectors (IVs) allowing an IV attack to discover the key.

A is incorrect. SSL uses RC4 successfully to encrypt and decrypt traffic but WEP does not use SSL.

C is incorrect. CCMP is a strong encryption protocol based on AES that overcomes problems with TKIP and WEP did not use CCMP.

D is incorrect. AES is a strong encryption standard, WEP did not use AES.

Objective: 3.4 Analyze and differentiate among types of wireless attacks

26. While troubleshooting a problem with a WAP in your organization, you discover a rogue access point with the same SSID as the organization's WAP. What is this second access point?

    A. IDS

    B. War chalking

    C. Evil twin

    D. Packet sniffer

26. **C** is correct. An evil twin is a rogue (or counterfeit) access point with the same SSID as an authorized wireless access point (WAP).

A is incorrect. An IDS detects malicious activity after it has occurred, but is unrelated to WAPs.

B is incorrect. War chalking is the practice of drawing symbols in public places to identify wireless networks.

D is incorrect. While the evil twin is very likely capturing traffic with packet sniffing, an evil twin is not a packet sniffer.

Objective: 3.4 Analyze and differentiate among types of wireless attacks

27. You want to identify the physical location of a rogue access point you discovered in the footprint of your company. What would you use?

    A. Bluesnarfing

    B. Bluejacking

    C. War chalking

    D. War driving

27. **D** is correct. War driving is the practice of looking for a wireless network, and administrators sometimes use war driving as part of a wireless audit to locate rogue access points.

A is incorrect. Bluesnarfing involves accessing data on a phone.

B is incorrect. Bluejacking involves sending unsolicited messages to a phone.

C is incorrect. War chalking identifies publically accessible wireless networks with symbols written in chalk, or painted on a wall as graffiti.

Objective: 3.4 Analyze and differentiate among types of wireless attacks

28. You are hosting a wireless hotspot and you want to segment each wireless user from each other. What should you use?

    A. Personal mode

    B. Enterprise mode

    C. Isolation mode

    D. WEP

28. **C** is correct. Isolation mode on a WAP segments wireless users from each other and is commonly used in hotspots.

A and B are incorrect. Personal mode uses a PSK and Enterprise mode uses an 802.1X authentication server to increase security.

D is incorrect. WEP is a weak encryption algorithm and not recommended for use.

Objective: 3.4 Analyze and differentiate among types of wireless attacks

29. Which of the following best describes bluejacking?

    A. Bluejacking involves accessing data on a phone.

    B. Bluejacking involves checking a WAPs antenna placement, power levels, and encryption techniques.

    C. Bluejacking involves sending unsolicited messages to a phone.

    D. Bluejacking involves a rogue access point with the same SSID as your production WAP.

29. **C** is correct. Bluejacking involves sending unsolicited messages to a phone.

A is incorrect. Bluesnarfing involves accessing data on a phone.

B is incorrect. A wireless audit involves checking a WAPs antenna placement, power levels, and encryption techniques.

D is incorrect. An evil twin is a rogue access point with the same SSID as an authorized WAP.

Objective: 3.4 Analyze and differentiate among types of wireless attacks

30. Your organization wants to reduce threats from zero day vulnerabilities. Of the following choices, what provides the best solution?

    A. Opening ports on a server's firewall

    B. Disabling unnecessary services

    C. Keep systems up-to-date with current patches

    D. Keep systems up-to-date with current service packs

30. **B** is correct. Disabling unnecessary services helps reduce threats, including threats from zero day vulnerabilities.

A is incorrect. It also reduces the threat from open ports on a firewall if the associated services are disabled, but opening ports won't reduce threats.

C is incorrect. Keeping systems up to date with patches and service packs protects against known vulnerabilities and is certainly a good practice.

D is incorrect. However, by definition there aren't any patches or service packs available for zero day vulnerabilities.

Objective: 3.5 Analyze and differentiate among types of application attacks

31. What can a header manipulation attack modify?

    A. Flags

    B. Buffers

    C. Databases

    D. Signature definitions

31. **A** is correct. A header manipulation modifies flags and data in a packet and can launch a session hijacking attack.

B is incorrect. Buffer overflow attacks can modify memory buffers.

C is incorrect. SQL injection attacks can modify databases.

D is incorrect. Antivirus software requires up-to-date signature definitions, but header manipulation does not modify these.

Objective: 3.5 Analyze and differentiate among types of application attacks

32. An IDS detected a NOOP sled. What kind of attack does this indicate?

    A. Input validation

    B. SQL injection

    C. Cross-site scripting

    D. Buffer overflow

32. **D** is correct. Many buffer overflow attacks use a string of no operation commands as a NOOP sled, and while input validation prevents a buffer overflow attack, an intrusion detection system (IDS) can detect them.

A is incorrect. Input validation checks input data and can help mitigate buffer overflow, SQL injection, and cross-site scripting attacks.

B is incorrect. SQL injection attacks use SQL statements.

C is incorrect. Cross-site scripting attacks use HTML or JavaScript tags.

Objective: 3.5 Analyze and differentiate among types of application attacks

33. A web-based application expects a user to enter eight characters into a text box. However, the application allows a user to copy more than eight characters into the text box. What is a potential vulnerability for this application?

    A. Input validation

    B. Buffer overflow

    C. SYN flood

    D. Flood guard

33. **B** is correct. A buffer overflow occurs when an application receives more data than it expects and can expose system memory.

A is incorrect. Input validation checks input data and can help mitigate buffer overflow, SQL injection, and cross-site scripting attacks.

C and D are incorrect. A SYN flood attack withholds the third packet in a TCP handshake and a flood guard is a security control that protects against SYN flood attacks.

Objective: 3.5 Analyze and differentiate among types of application attacks

34. While analyzing an application log, you discover several entries where a user has entered the following command into a web-based form: ../etc/passwd. What does this indicate?

    A. Fuzzing

    B. Kiting

    C. Command injection attack

    D. DoS

34. **C** is correct. A command injection attack is any attempt to inject commands into an application such as a web-based form and in this case, the attack is attempting to retrieve password information with directory traversal.

A is incorrect. Fuzzing, or fuzz testing, sends invalid, unexpected, or random data to a system and can detect buffer overflow vulnerabilities.

B is incorrect. Kiting is the practice of repeatedly reserving domain names without paying for them.

D is incorrect. A DDoS attack is launched from multiple computers and results in loss of services.

Objective: 3.5 Analyze and differentiate among types of application attacks

35. What will protect against a SYN attack?

    A. Input validation

    B. Error handling

    C. Flood guard

    D. Cross-site scripting

35. **C** is correct. Flood guards help protect against SYN flood attacks.

A is incorrect. Input validation checks input data and can help mitigate buffer overflow, SQL injection, and cross-site scripting attacks.

B is incorrect. Error handling routines are a part of input validation and can prevent application failures and many application attacks.

D is incorrect. Cross-site scripting is an attack that uses HTML or JavaScript tags.

Objective: 3.6 Analyze and differentiate among types of mitigation and deterrent techniques

36. What can an administrator use to detect a DDoS attack?

    A. Privilege escalation

    B. Performance baseline

    C. Web form sanitization

    D. Antivirus software

36. **B** is correct. A performance baseline can help detect a Distributed Denial of Service (DDoS) by showing differences in performance.

A is incorrect. Malware uses privilege escalation to gain more rights and permissions after compromising a system.

C is incorrect. Web form sanitization (or input validation) can prevent injection attacks, but won't detect a DDoS attack.

D is incorrect. Antivirus software can detect viruses, worms, and Trojan horses, but not DDoS attacks.

Objective: 3.6 Analyze and differentiate among types of mitigation and deterrent techniques

37. You want to check a log to determine when a user logged on and off of a system. What log would you check?

    A. System

    B. Application

    C. Firewall

    D. Security

37. **D** is correct. The Security log records auditable events such as user logons and logoffs.

A is incorrect. The System log records system such as when a service stops and starts.

B is incorrect. The Application log records events from individual applications.

C is incorrect. A firewall log can record what traffic is passed and what traffic is blocked.

Objective: 3.6 Analyze and differentiate among types of mitigation and deterrent techniques

38. Which of the following is a preventative control that can prevent outages due to ad-hoc configuration errors?

    A. Least privilege

    B. A periodic review of user rights

    C. Change management plan

    D. Security audit

38. **C** is correct. A change management strategy can prevent outages by ensuring that configuration changes aren't made on an as needed (ad-hoc) basis, but instead are examined prior to making the change; change management is also known as an operational control.

A and B are incorrect. The principle of least privilege is a technical control and ensures that users only have the rights and permissions needed to perform the job, and no more.

D is incorrect. A security audit is a detective control and a periodic review of user rights is a specific type of detective control.

Objective: 3.6 Analyze and differentiate among types of mitigation and deterrent techniques

39. Which of the following is a preventative control?

    A. Least privilege

    B. Security audit

    C. Security guard

    D. Periodic review of user rights

39. **C** is correct. A security guard (armed or not armed) is a preventative physical security control.

A is incorrect. The principle of least privilege is a technical control and ensures that users only have the rights and permissions needed to perform the job, and no more.

B and D are incorrect. A security audit is a detective control and a periodic review of user rights is a specific type of detective control.

Objective: 3.6 Analyze and differentiate among types of mitigation and deterrent techniques

40. Your organization regularly performs routine security audits to assess the security posture. What type of control is this?

    A. Corrective

    B. Technical

    C. Detective

    D. Preventative

40. **C** is correct. A security audit is a form of detective control since it will detect when a vulnerability has been exploited after the fact.

A is incorrect. A corrective control attempts to reverse the effects of a problem.

B is incorrect. A technical control (such as the principle of least privilege) enforces security using technical means.

D is incorrect. A preventative control attempts to prevent an incident from occurring.

Objective: 3.6 Analyze and differentiate among types of mitigation and deterrent techniques

41. Of the following choices, what is a detective security control?

    A. Change management

    B. HVAC

    C. CCTV

    D. User training

41. **C** is correct. A closed circuit television (CCTV) system can record activity and can detect what occurred as a detective security control.

A is incorrect. Change management is a preventative control.

B is incorrect. HVAC is an environmental control that is preventative.

D is incorrect. User training is preventative.

Objective: 3.6 Analyze and differentiate among types of mitigation and deterrent techniques

42. What is the purpose of a cipher lock system?

    A. Control door access with a keypad

    B. Control door access with a proximity card

    C. Control access to a laptop with biometrics

    D. Control access to laptop with a smart card.

42. A is correct. A cipher lock system is a door access security method and only opens after a user has entered the correct code into the cipher lock.

B is incorrect. A proximity card uses a proximity card reader, not a cipher lock.

C and D are incorrect. Biometric readers (such as a fingerprint reader) and smart cards can be used as authentication for systems such as laptop systems.

Objective: 3.6 Analyze and differentiate among types of mitigation and deterrent techniques

43. What can you use to electronically unlock a door for specific users?

    A. Token

    B. Proximity card

    C. Physical key

    D. Certificate

43. B is correct. Proximity cards are used as an additional access control in some areas to electronically unlock doors.

A is incorrect. A token (such as an RSA token) provides a rolling password for one-time use.

C is incorrect. A physical key does not electronically unlock a door.

D is incorrect. A certificate can be embedded in a smart card but by itself, it would not electronically unlock a door.

Objective: 3.6 Analyze and differentiate among types of mitigation and deterrent techniques

44. An organization wants to prevent unauthorized personnel from entering a secure workspace. Of the following choices, what can be used? (Choose two).

    A. Security guard

    B. Piggybacking

    C. CCTV

    D. Proximity cards

44. **A** and **D** are correct. Security guards and proximity cards are valid methods to prevent unauthorized personnel from entering a secure workspace such as a secure datacenter.

B is incorrect. Piggybacking (also called tailgating) occurs when one user follows closely behind another user without using credentials and can be prevented with a mantrap.

C is incorrect. A CCTV can detect if an unauthorized entry occurred and provide reliable proof of the entry, but it can't prevent it.

Objective: 3.6 Analyze and differentiate among types of mitigation and deterrent techniques

45. A company hosts a datacenter with highly sensitive data. Of the following choices, what can provide the best type of physical security to prevent unauthorized entry?

    A. Proximity card

    B. CCTV

    C. ID badges

    D. Mantrap

45. **D** is correct. A mantrap is highly effective at preventing unauthorized entry and can also be used to prevent tailgating.

A is incorrect. A proximity card is useful as an access control mechanism, but it won't prevent tailgating so it isn't as useful as a mantrap.

B is incorrect. CCTV provides video surveillance and it can record unauthorized entry, but it can't prevent it.

C is incorrect. ID badges are useful if the entry is staffed with security guards, but won't prevent unauthorized entry if used without security guards.

Objective: 3.6 Analyze and differentiate among types of mitigation and deterrent techniques

46. You are evaluating the security and availability of a system. Security is more important than availability in the system. If it fails, what state should it fail in?

    A. It should fail open

    B. It should fail closed

    C. It should shut down

D. It should be rebooted

46. **B** is correct. If security is more important than availability, it should fail in a closed state.

A is incorrect. If availability is more important than security, it should fail in an open state.

C and D are incorrect. Different systems can achieve a closed state using different methods and they don't necessarily have to be shut down or rebooted.

Objective: 3.6 Analyze and differentiate among types of mitigation and deterrent techniques

47. Two employees have entered a secure datacenter. However, only one employee provided credentials. How did the other employee gain entry?

    A. Mantrap

    B. HVAC

    C. Vishing

    D. Tailgating

47. **D** is correct. Tailgating (also called piggybacking) occurs when one user follows closely behind another user without using credentials.

A is incorrect. A mantrap prevents tailgating.

B is incorrect. A Heating, Ventilation, and Air Conditioning (HVAC) system can increase availability by ensuring that equipment doesn't fail due to overheating.

C is incorrect. Vishing is a variant of phishing techniques and often combines social engineering tactics with Voice over IP (VoIP).

Objective: 3.6 Analyze and differentiate among types of mitigation and deterrent techniques

48. You have recently added a server to your network that will host data used and updated by employees. You want to monitor security events on the system. Of the following, what is the most important security event to monitor?

    A. Data modifications

    B. TCP connections

    C. UDP connections

    D. Account logon attempts

48. **D** is correct. Of the choices, account logon attempts are the most important.

A is incorrect. Since the purpose of the system is to host data that is read and updated by employees, data modifications are not critical because they are expected to occur regularly.

B and C are incorrect. TCP and UDP are the primary protocols used when users connect to a server over a network, but it's not important from a security perspective to monitor these events.

Objective: 3.6 Analyze and differentiate among types of mitigation and deterrent techniques

49. What is included in a risk assessment? (Choose three.)

    A. Threats

    B. Vulnerabilities

    C. Asset values

    D. Recommendations to eliminate risk

49. **A, B,** and **C** are correct. A risk assessment identifies assets, asset values, threats, and vulnerabilities. It prioritizes the results and makes recommendations on what controls to implement.

D is incorrect. Risk cannot be eliminated.

Objective: 3.7 Implement assessment tools and techniques to discover security threats and vulnerabilities

50. Which of the following statements are true regarding risk assessments? (Choose two.)

    A. A quantitative risk assessment uses hard numbers.

    B. A qualitative risk assessment uses on hard numbers.

    C. A qualitative risk assessment uses a subjective ranking.

    D. A quantitative risk assessment uses a subjective ranking.

50. **A** and **C** are correct. A quantitative risk assessment uses hard numbers (such as costs) and a qualitative risk assessment uses a subjective ranking based on judgments.

B is incorrect. A qualitative risk assessment does not use hard numbers'

D is incorrect. A quantitative risk assessment does not use subjective rankings.

Objective: 3.7 Implement assessment tools and techniques to discover security threats and vulnerabilities

51. A security professional is performing a qualitative risk analysis. Of the following choices, what will most likely to be used in the assessment?

    A. Cost

    B. Judgment

    C. ALE

    D. Hard numbers

51. **B** is correct. A qualitative risk assessment uses judgment to categorize risks based on probability and impact.

A and D are incorrect. A quantitative risk assessment uses hard numbers such as costs and asset values.

C is incorrect. A quantitative risk assessment uses annual loss expectancy (ALE).

Objective: 3.7 Implement assessment tools and techniques to discover security threats and vulnerabilities

52. An organization recently completed a risk assessment. Who should be granted access to the report?

    A. All employees

    B. Security professionals only

    C. Executive management only

    D. Security professionals and executive management

52. **D** is correct. Executive management needs access to the report to approve controls and security professionals need access to the report to implement the controls.

A is incorrect. The report has sensitive data and should not be released to all employees.

B is incorrect. The report is also needed by security professionals so should not be released only to executive management.

C is incorrect. The report is also needed by executive management so should not be released only to security professionals.

Objective: 3.7 Implement assessment tools and techniques to discover security threats and vulnerabilities

53. A security administrator is performing a vulnerability assessment. Which of the following actions would be included?

    A. Implement a password policy

    B. Delete unused accounts

    C. Organize data based on severity and asset value

    D. Remove system rights for users that don't need them

53. **C** is correct. The vulnerability assessment is prioritized based on the severity of the vulnerabilities and their ability to affect the high value asset items.

A, B, and D are incorrect. A vulnerability assessment checks for the existence of security controls such as a password policy and can include a user rights and access review to identify unused accounts, or accounts with unneeded permissions. However, a vulnerability assessment identifies these issues, but does not make changes.

Objective: 3.7 Implement assessment tools and techniques to discover security threats and vulnerabilities

54. An organization has released an application. Of the following choices, what is the most thorough way to discover vulnerabilities with the application?

    A. Fuzzing

    B. OVAL comparison

    C. Rainbow table

    D. Code review

54. **D** is correct. A code review is a line-by-line examination of the code to discover vulnerabilities and is the most thorough of the choices.

A is incorrect. Fuzzing sends random data to an application to identify vulnerabilities but it will generally only find simple problems and isn't as thorough as a code review.

B is incorrect. The Open Vulnerability and Assessment Language (OVAL) is an international standard used to rate the exposure of vulnerabilities, but doesn't discover them.

C is incorrect. A rainbow table is a lookup table used to crack weak passwords.

Objective: 3.7 Implement assessment tools and techniques to discover security threats and vulnerabilities

55. Which of the following tools can perform a port scan? (Choose all that apply.)

    A. Nmap

    B. Netcat

    C. Wireshark

    D. Netstat

55. **A** and **B** are correct. Nmap and Netcat are two tools that can perform port scans and vulnerability scans.

C is incorrect. Wireshark is a protocol analyzer and can view headers and clear-text contents in IP packets.

D is incorrect. Netstat is a command-line tool that identifies open connections.

Objective: 3.7 Implement assessment tools and techniques to discover security threats and vulnerabilities

56. What can you use to examine IP headers in a data packet?

    A. Protocol analyzer

    B. Port scanner

    C. Vulnerability scanner

    D. Penetration tester

56. **A** is correct. You can use a protocol analyzer (sniffer) to view headers and clear-text contents in IP packets.

B is incorrect. A port scanner can detect open ports.

C and D are incorrect. A vulnerability scanner will passively identify vulnerabilities and a penetration will actively try to exploit vulnerabilities, and even though some may examine IP headers, not all of them do.

Objective: 3.7 Implement assessment tools and techniques to discover security threats and vulnerabilities

57. What can you use to examine text transmitted over a network by an application?

    A. Honeypot

    B. Honeynet

    C. Protocol analyzer

    D. Vulnerability scanner

57. **C** is correct. You can use a protocol analyzer (sniffer) to view headers and clear-text contents in IP packets.

A and B are incorrect. A honeypot is a system used to divert an attacker from a live network and a honeynet is a group of honeypots.

D is incorrect. A vulnerability scanner will passively identify vulnerabilities but doesn't always include the ability examine transmitted text.

Objective: 3.7 Implement assessment tools and techniques to discover security threats and vulnerabilities

58. An administrator suspects that a computer is sending out large amounts of sensitive data to an external system. What tool can the administrator use to verify this?

A. Rainbow table

B. Protocol analyzer

C. Password cracker

D. Port scanner

58. **B** is correct. A protocol analyzer can capture packets and view the contents including data sent across the network.

A and C are incorrect. A rainbow table is a lookup table used by password crackers to crack weak passwords, and a password cracker cracks passwords.

D is incorrect. A port scanner identifies open ports on a system.

Objective: 3.7 Implement assessment tools and techniques to discover security threats and vulnerabilities

59. An administrator suspects that a web application is sending database credentials across the network in clear text. What can the administrator use to verify this?

A. SQL injection

B. Protocol analyzer

C. A network-based DLP

D. Password cracker

59. **B** is correct. A protocol analyzer can capture packets and view the contents, including credentials sent across the network in clear text.

A is incorrect. SQL injection is an attack against a database through an application that isn't using input validation.

C is incorrect. A network-based data loss prevention (DLP) system can examine and analyze email and detect if confidential company data is included.

D is incorrect. A password cracker cracks passwords that are protected, not that are sent in clear-text.

Objective: 3.7 Implement assessment tools and techniques to discover security threats and vulnerabilities

60. Sally used WinZip to create an archive of several sensitive documents on an upcoming merger and she password-protected the archive file. Of the following choices, what is the best way to test the security of the archive file?

    A. Rainbow table

    B. Vulnerability scanner

    C. Password cracker

    D. Sniffer

60. **C** is correct. A password cracker can attempt to crack the password of a password-protected file and is the best choice here.

A is incorrect. Some password crackers use a rainbow table, but it can't be used by itself.

B is incorrect. A vulnerability scanner can scan for vulnerabilities, but it won't necessarily be able to check for a password for an archive file.

D is incorrect. You can use a sniffer (protocol analyzer) to view headers and clear-text contents in IP packets.

Objective: 3.7 Implement assessment tools and techniques to discover security threats and vulnerabilities

61. Of the following choices, what can you use to divert malicious attacks on your network away from valuable resources to relatively worthless resources?

    A. IDS

    B. Proxy server

    C. Web application firewall

    D. Honeypot

61. **D** is correct. A honeypot can divert malicious attacks to a harmless area of your network, away from production servers.

A is incorrect. An IDS can detect attacks, but only an active IDS (or an IPS) will take action, and it usually blocks the attack instead of diverting it.

B is incorrect. A proxy server can filter and cache content from web pages, but doesn't divert attacks.

C is incorrect. A web application firewall (WAF) is an additional firewall designed to protect a web application.

Objective: 3.7 Implement assessment tools and techniques to discover security threats and vulnerabilities

62. An organization develops its own software. Of the following choices what is a security practice that should be included in the process?

    A. Check vendor documentation

    B. SDLC Waterfall model

    C. Code review

    D. Enabling command injection

62. **C** is correct. Secure software development includes security at each stage of development including code reviews for security.

A is incorrect. Vendor documentation for purchased software is an important application-hardening step, but in-house developed software wouldn't have vendor documentation during development.

B is incorrect. Using an SDLC model helps an organization manage the development process, but there is nothing in the question to indicate that the Waterfall model should be used.

D is incorrect. Attacks use command injection and applications should block command injection.

Objective: 3.7 Implement assessment tools and techniques to discover security threats and vulnerabilities

63. You are trying to determine what systems on your network are most susceptible to an attack. What tool would you use?

    A. Port scanner

    B. SQL injection

    C. Header manipulation

    D. Vulnerability scanner

63. **D** is correct. A vulnerability scanner can scan systems for vulnerabilities and determine which ones are most susceptible to an attack.

A is incorrect. A port scanner scans a system for open ports and helps identify what services are running.

B is incorrect. SQL injection is a narrow attack on databases but it would not check all systems.

C is incorrect. Attackers can manipulate headers in TCP packets for specific attacks, but this isn't as useful as a vulnerability scanner.

Objective: 3.8 Within the realm of vulnerability assessments, explain the proper use of penetration testing versus vulnerability scanning

64. A security administrator used a tool to discover security issues, but did not exploit them. What best describes this action?

    A. Penetration test

    B. Vulnerability scan

    C. Protocol analysis

    D. Port scan

64. **B** is correct. A vulnerability scan attempts to discover vulnerabilities but does not exploit them.

A is incorrect. A penetration test actively tests security controls by trying to exploit vulnerabilities.

C is incorrect. A protocol analyzer can capture and analyze IP packets but isn't as useful as a vulnerability scanner to discover security issues.

D is incorrect. A port scanner will identify open ports but won't identify security issues.

Objective: 3.8 Within the realm of vulnerability assessments, explain the proper use of penetration testing versus vulnerability scanning

65. An administrator needs to test the security of a network without affecting normal operations. What can the administrator use?

    A. Internal penetration test

    B. External penetration test

C. Vulnerability scanner

D. Protocol analyzer

65. **C** is correct. A vulnerability scanner will test the security of the network without affecting users.

A and B are incorrect. A penetration test (external or internal) is active and can affect users.

D is incorrect. A protocol analyzer can capture and analyze IP packets but won't test the security of a network.

Objective: 3.8 Within the realm of vulnerability assessments, explain the proper use of penetration testing versus vulnerability scanning

66. A security administrator wants to scan the network for a wide range of potential security and configuration issues. What tool provides this service?

A. Fuzzer

B. Protocol analyzer

C. Port scanner

D. Vulnerability scanner

66. **D** is correct. A vulnerability scanner is a management control that can identify a wide range of security and configuration issues.

A is incorrect. A fuzzer is an active tool that sends random data to a system and can potentially result in an outage.

B and C are incorrect. A protocol analyzer can capture and analyze IP packets and a port scanner can identify open ports. However, the question is asking for a tool that can scan the network for a wide range of issues, and vulnerability scanners can do more than either a protocol analyzer or a port scanner.

Objective: 3.8 Within the realm of vulnerability assessments, explain the proper use of penetration testing versus vulnerability scanning

67. A security professional is performing a penetration test on a system. Of the following choices, what identifies the best description of what this will accomplish?

    A. Passively detect vulnerabilities

    B. Actively assess security controls

    C. Identify lack of security controls

    D. Identify common misconfiguration

67. **B** is correct. A penetration test will actively assess or test security controls.

A, C, and D are incorrect. A vulnerability scan is passive and detects vulnerabilities, identifies a lack of security controls, and identifies common misconfigurations but it stops there. Further, the three incorrect answers are specifically listed under Vulnerability scanning in the objectives as:

Passively testing security controls

Identify vulnerability

Identify lack of security controls

Identify common misconfiguration

While a penetration test starts with a passive vulnerability scan, it goes a step further to actively test the controls.

Objective: 3.8 Within the realm of vulnerability assessments, explain the proper use of penetration testing versus vulnerability scanning

68. An organization is hiring a security firm to perform vulnerability testing. What should they define before the testing?

    A. Rules of engagement

    B. Information given to the black box testers

    C. Vulnerabilities

    D. Existing security controls

68. **A** is correct. A rules of engagement document identifies boundaries of a test and expectations of the testers, and it provides consent for the testers to perform the test.

B is incorrect. Black box testers are not given any knowledge prior to the test.

C is incorrect. The test will help identify vulnerabilities so these aren't defined before the test.

D is incorrect. It's not required to tell the testers what security controls are in place.

Objective: 3.8 Within the realm of vulnerability assessments, explain the proper use of penetration testing versus vulnerability scanning

69. An organization wants to test how well employees can respond to a compromised system. Of the following choices, what identifies the best choice to test the response?

    A. Vulnerability scan

    B. White hat test

    C. Black hat test

    D. Penetration test

69. **D** is correct. A penetration test will exploit vulnerabilities and will test employee's ability to respond to a compromised system.

A is incorrect. A vulnerability scan will identify vulnerabilities but not exploit them so employees won't need to respond.

B is incorrect. White hat refers to a security professional working within the law and black hat refers to a malicious attacker, but these aren't tests.

C is incorrect. Black box testing, white box testing, and gray box testing (not included in the answers) are forms of penetration testing.

Objective: 3.8 Within the realm of vulnerability assessments, explain the proper use of penetration testing versus vulnerability scanning

70. Testers have access to product documentation and source code for an application that they are using in a vulnerability test. What type of test is this?

    A. Black box

    B. White box

    C. Black hat

    D. White hat

70. **B** is correct. In white box testing, testers have access to all of the system details.

A is incorrect. In a black box test, testers have zero knowledge of system details.

C and D are incorrect. Black hat identifies a malicious attacker while white hat identifies a security professional working within the bounds of the law.

Objective: 3.8 Within the realm of vulnerability assessments, explain the proper use of penetration testing versus vulnerability scanning

71. A tester is fuzzing an application. What is another name for this?

    A. Black box testing

    B. White box testing

    C. Gray box testing

    D. Black hat testing

71. **A** is correct. Fuzzing sends random data to an application and is sometimes referred to as black box testing.

B and C are incorrect. White box and gray box testing have some knowledge of the application and can test the application with specific data rather than random data.

D is incorrect. Black hat refers to a malicious attacker not a tester, though a black hat attacker can use a fuzzer.

Objective: 3.8 Within the realm of vulnerability assessments, explain the proper use of penetration testing versus vulnerability scanning.

Chapter 4 Application, Data and Host Security

Application, Data, and Host Security topics are **16 percent** of the CompTIA Security+ exam. The objectives in this domain are:

4.1 Explain the importance of application security

- Fuzzing
- Secure coding concepts
    - o Error and exception handling
    - o Input validation
- Cross-site scripting prevention
- Cross-site Request Forgery (XSRF) prevention
- Application configuration baseline (proper settings)
- Application hardening
- Application patch management

4.2 Carry out appropriate procedures to establish host security

- Operating system security and settings
- Anti-malware
    - o Anti-virus
    - o Anti-spam
    - o Anti-spyware
    - o Pop-up blockers
    - o Host-based firewalls
- Patch management
- Hardware security
    - o Cable locks
    - o Safe
    - o Locking cabinets
- Host software baselining
- Mobile devices
    - o Screen lock

- o   Strong password
- o   Device encryption
- o   Remote wipe/sanitation
- o   Voice encryption
- o   GPS tracking
- Virtualization

4.3 Explain the importance of data security
- Data Loss Prevention (DLP)
- Data encryption
  - o   Full disk
  - o   Database
  - o   Individual files
  - o   Removable media
  - o   Mobile devices
- Hardware based encryption devices
  - o   TPM
  - o   HSM
  - o   USB encryption
  - o   Hard drive
- Cloud computing

The CompTIA Security+: Get Certified Get Ahead SY0-301 Study Guide (ISBN 1463762364) discusses these topics in much more depth. Sec-plus.com has more details on the availability of this book.

√ **Get Certified**
  √ **Get Ahead**

Practice Test Questions for Application, Data and Host Security Domain

1. You manage a server hosting a third-party database application. You want to ensure that the application is secure and all unnecessary services are disabled. What should you perform?

    A. Secure code review

    B. Application hardening

    C. White box testing

    D. White hat testing

2. Of the following choices, what is a step used to harden a database application?

    A. Enabling all services

    B. Disabling default accounts and changing default passwords

    C. Disabling SQL

    D. Disabling stored procedures

3. An attacker is entering incorrect data into a form on a web page. The result shows the attacker the type of database used by the website and provides hints on what SQL statements the database accepts. What can prevent this?

    A. Error handling

    B. Antivirus software

    C. Antispam software

    D. Flood guards

4. Your organization hosts several websites accessible on the Internet, and is conducting a security review of these sites. Of the following choices, what is the most common security issue for web-based applications?

    A. Input validation

    B. Phishing

    C. Whaling

    D. Social engineering

5. Of the following choices, what can help prevent SQL injection attacks?

    A. Output validation

    B. NOOP sleds

    C. Stored procedures

    D. Antivirus software

6. A web developer wants to prevent cross-site scripting. What should the developer do?

    A. Use input validation to remove hypertext

    B. Use input validation to remove cookies

    C. Use input validation to SQL statements

    D. Use input validation to overflow buffers

7. A website prevents users from using the less than character (<)when entering data into forms. What are they trying to prevent?

    A. Logic bomb

    B. Cross-site scripting

    C. Fuzzing

    D. SQL injection

8. What can an attacker use to identify vulnerabilities in an application?

    A. Protocol analyzer

    B. Port scanner

    C. Fuzzing

    D. IPS

9. An attacker recently used a SQL injection attack against a company's web site. How can the company prevent future SQL injection attacks?

    A. Add SSL encryption

    B. Add input validation

    C. Add antivirus software

    D. Add cross-site scripting capabilities

10. Of the following choices, what could you use to deploy baseline security configurations to multiple systems?

    A. IDS

    B. Security template

    C. Change management

    D. Performance baseline

11. An administrator wants to prevent users from installing software. Of the following choices, what is the easiest way to accomplish this?

    A. Manually remove administrative rights

    B. Implement port scanners

    C. Use a security template

    D. Implement a job rotation policy

12. You are troubleshooting a server that users claim is running slow. You notice that the server frequently has about 20 active SSH sessions. What can you use to determine if this is normal behavior?

    A. Vendor documentation

    B. Security template

    C. Baseline report

    D. Imaging

13. Your organization is considering deploying multiple servers using a standardized image. Of the following choices, what best describes the security benefit of this plan?

    A. The image can include unnecessary protocols

    B. The image provides fault tolerance as a RAID 5

    C. It eliminates Trojans

    D. The image can include mandated security configurations

14. Management is reviewing a hardware inventory in a datacenter. They realize that many of the servers are underutilized resulting in wasted resources. What can they do to improve the situation?

    A. Implement virtualization

    B. Implement VM escape

    C. Increase the datacenter footprint

    D. Add TPMs

15. You have created an image for a database server that you plan to deploy to five physical servers. At the last minute, management decides to deploy these as virtual servers. What additional security steps do you need to take with these virtual images before deploying them?

    A. None

    B. Lock down the virtual images

    C. Install virtual antivirus software

    D. Install virtual patches

16. Of the following choices, what indicates the best method of reducing operating system vulnerabilities?

    A. Whole disk encryption

    B. Patch management

    C. Trusted Platform Module

    D. File level encryption

17. Of the following choices, what would you use in a patch management process?

    A. VM escape

    B. TPM

    C. Penetration testing

    D. Regression testing

18. An organization recently suffered a significant outage due to attacks on unpatched systems. Investigation showed that administrators did not have a clear idea of when they should apply the patches. What can they do to prevent a reoccurrence of this problem?

    A. Apply all patches immediately

    B. Apply the missing patches on the attacked systems immediately

    C. Test the patches with regression testing in a test environment mirroring the production environment

    D. Create a patch management policy

19. Additional windows are appearing when a user surfs the Internet. These aren't malicious but the user wants them to stop. What can stop this behavior?

    A. Antivirus software

    B. Host-based firewall

    C. Pop-up blocker

    D. Input validation

20. What type of signature-based monitoring can detect and remove known worms and Trojans?

    A. Antispyware

    B. NIDS

    C. NIPS

    D. Antivirus

21. A user's computer has recently been slower than normal and has been sending out email without user interaction. Of the following choices, what is the best choice to resolve this issue?

    A. Botnet software

    B. Antispam software

    C. Anti-spyware software

    D. Antivirus software

22. What can reduce unwanted email that contains advertisements?

    A. Antispam software

    B. Antivirus software

    C. File integrity checkers

    D. Botnet software

23. Someone stole an executive's smart phone and the phone includes sensitive data. What should you do to prevent the thief from reading the data?

    A. Password protect the phone

    B. Encrypt the data on the phone

    C. Use remote wipe

D. Track the location of the phone

24. What can you use to block unsolicited email?

A. Spam filter

B. Rootkit

C. Spyware

D. Antivirus software

25. Your organization has several portable USB drives that users are able to use to transfer large video files instead of copying them over the network. What should be used to prevent the theft of these drives when they are not being used?

A. HSM

B. TPM

C. Video surveillance

D. Locked cabinet

26. A company prohibits the use of USB flash drives to prevent data leakage. Of the following choices, what could the company also do to reduce data leakage?

A. Prohibit personal music devices

B. Remove labels from backup media

C. Prohibit the storage of backups off-site

D. Prohibit DLP devices

27. A file server within a network hosts files that employees throughout the company regularly access. Management wants to ensure that some personnel files on this server are not accessible by administrators. What provides the best protection?

    A. Remove administrative access to the server

    B. Protect the files with permissions

    C. Use file encryption

    D. Use full disk encryption

28. You organization is considering purchasing new computers that include hardware encryption capabilities. What benefit does this provide?

    A. It is faster than software encryption

    B. It does not require a TPM

    C. It does not require an HSM

    D. Reduced confidentiality

29. Your organization recently purchased several new laptop computers for employees. You're asked to encrypt the laptop's hard drives without purchasing any additional hardware. What would you use?

    A. TPM

    B. HSM

    C. VM escape

    D. DLP

30. Your organization is considering the purchase of new computers. A security professional stresses that these devices should include TPMs. What benefit does a TPM provide? (Choose all that apply.)

    A. It use hardware encryption, which is quicker than software encryption

    B. It use software encryption, which is quicker than hardware encryption

    C. It includes an HSM file system

    D. It stores RSA keys

31. Of the following choices, what is the best choice to provide encryption services in a clustered environment?

    A. Virtual servers

    B. SaaS provider

    C. HSM

    D. TPM

32. What functions does an HSM include?

    A. Reduces the risk of employees emailing confidential information outside the organization

    B. Provides webmail to clients

    C. Provides full drive encryption

    D. Generates and store keys

33. Employees regularly send email in and out of the company. The company suspects that some employees are sending out confidential data and they want to take steps to reduce this risk. What can they use?

    A. HSM

    B. TPM

    C. A network-based DLP

    D. Port scanner

34. Your organization wants to prevent losses due to data leakage on portable devices. What provides the best protection?

A. Smart cards

    B. Full disk encryption

    C. Permissions

    D. SSH

35. Your organization has an existing server and you want to add a hardware device to provide encryption capabilities. What is the easiest way to accomplish this?

    A. TPM

    B. HSM

    C. DLP

    D. IaaS

36. Your organization issues laptop computers to employees. Employees use them while traveling, and frequently store sensitive data on these systems. What can you use to recover a laptop if an employee loses it?

A. Encryption

B. Remote wipe

C. Remote lock

D. GPS tracking

37. Of the following choices, what is a primary benefit of data labeling?

A. To identify data collected from a public web site

B. To prevent the handling of PII

C. To identify PII

D. Ensure that employees understand data they are handling

38. A company was recently involved in a legal issue that resulted in administrators spending a significant amount of time retrieving data from archives in response to a court order. The company wants to limit the time spent on similar events in the future. What can they do?

A. Implement separation of duties policies

B. Implement privacy policies

C. Create storage and retention policies

D. Perform user rights reviews

39. Of the following choices, what is the best way to protect the confidentiality of data?

A. Authentication

B. Encryption

C. Hashing

D. PaaS

40. An organization is disposing of old hard drives. What should security personnel do to prevent data leakage?

A. Sanitize the drive using bit level overwrites

B. Delete all data files

C. Format the drive

D. Remove operating system files

41. Organizations often restrict employee access of social networking sites from work locations. What are they trying to prevent?

A. Information disclosure

B. Employee morale

C. Risks from DoS attacks

D. Risks from DDoS attacks

42. Which of the following is PII when it is associated with a person's full name?

A. Pet's name

B. Birthdate

C. Favorite book

D. Favorite color

43. Why would an organization use information classification practices?

A. To enhance phishing

B. To enhance whaling

C. To protect sensitive data

D. To ensure PII is publically available

Practice Test Questions with Answers for Application, Data and Host Security Domain

1. You manage a server hosting a third-party database application. You want to ensure that the application is secure and all unnecessary services are disabled. What should you perform?

    A. Secure code review

    B. Application hardening

    C. White box testing

    D. White hat testing

1. **B** is correct. Application hardening ensures that a system is secure and includes basics such as disabling unnecessary services and checking vendor documentation.

A, C, and D are incorrect. The developer should perform secure code reviews and test the application before releasing it but these aren't steps for the customer of the application. In other words, the developer should have already performed these steps. Applications developed in-house (not third-party applications) require secure code reviews and third party black box testing is the most effective method of application testing.

Objective: 4.1 Explain the importance of application security

2. Of the following choices, what is a step used to harden a database application?

    A. Enabling all services

    B. Disabling default accounts and changing default passwords

C. Disabling SQL

D. Disabling stored procedures

2. **B** is correct. Application hardening (including hardening database applications) includes disabling default accounts and changing default passwords.

A is incorrect. Application hardening includes disabling unnecessary services, not enabling all of them.

C is incorrect. SQL is the language used to communicate with most databases so it shouldn't be disabled in a database application.

D is incorrect. Stored procedures increase performance, can help prevent SQL injection attacks, and shouldn't be disabled.

Objective: 4.1 Explain the importance of application security

3. An attacker is entering incorrect data into a form on a web page. The result shows the attacker the type of database used by the website and provides hints on what SQL statements the database accepts. What can prevent this?

A. Error handling

B. Antivirus software

C. Antispam software

D. Flood guards

3. **A** is correct. Error handling will return a generic error web page rather than a detailed error that can provide an attacker with valuable information to launch a SQL injection attack.

B is incorrect. Antivirus software can detect malware, such as viruses and worms, and prevent it from running on a computer.

C is incorrect. Antispam software can filter out unwanted or unsolicited email (also called spam).

D is incorrect. Flood guards can prevent SYN flood attacks.

Objective: 4.1 Explain the importance of application security

4. Your organization hosts several websites accessible on the Internet, and is conducting a security review of these sites. Of the following choices, what is the most common security issue for web-based applications?

    A. Input validation

    B. Phishing

    C. Whaling

    D. Social engineering

4. **A** is correct. Input validation checks input data, but because so many sites do not use it they are vulnerable to buffer overflow, SQL injection, and cross-site scripting attacks.

B is incorrect. Phishing is the practice of sending email to users with the purpose of tricking them into revealing personal information (such as bank account information).

C is incorrect. Whaling is a phishing attack that targets high-level executives.

D is incorrect. Social engineering is the practice of using social tactics to encourage a person to do something or reveal some piece of information.

Objective: 4.1 Explain the importance of application security

5. Of the following choices, what can help prevent SQL injection attacks?

    A. Output validation

    B. NOOP sleds

    C. Stored procedures

    D. Antivirus software

5. **C** is correct. Stored procedures help prevent SQL injection attacks by interpreting and validating inputted data rather than just using it in a SQL statement.

A is incorrect. Input validation (not output validation) is another method used to prevent SQL injection attacks.

B is incorrect. Many buffer overflow attacks use a string of no operation commands (NOOP sled).

D is incorrect. Antivirus software protects against malware but not SQL injection attacks.

Objective: 4.1 Explain the importance of application security

6. A web developer wants to prevent cross-site scripting. What should the developer do?

    A. Use input validation to remove hypertext

    B. Use input validation to remove cookies

    C. Use input validation to SQL statements

    D. Use input validation to overflow buffers

6. **A** is correct. Web developers reduce cross-site scripting attacks with input validation and filter out hypertext and JavaScript tags (using < and > characters).

B is incorrect. Cookies are text files used by the web site.

C is incorrect. SQL injection attacks use SQL statements and input validation helps prevent SQL injection attacks.

D is incorrect. Input validation can prevent buffer overflows reducing buffer overflow attacks.

Objective: 4.1 Explain the importance of application security

7. A website prevents users from using the less than character (<)when entering data into forms. What are they trying to prevent?

    A. Logic bomb

    B. Cross-site scripting

    C. Fuzzing

    D. SQL injection

7. **B** is correct. Web developers reduce cross-site scripting attacks with input validation and filtering out hypertext and JavaScript tags (using < and > characters).

A is incorrect. A logic bomb is a program or code snippet that executes in response to an event such as a specific time or date.

C is incorrect. Fuzzing sends pseudo-random data as input to an application in an attempt to crash or confuse it.

D is incorrect. Input validation blocks SQL injection attacks but SQL statements aren't blocked by blocking the < character.

Objective: 4.1 Explain the importance of application security

8. What can an attacker use to identify vulnerabilities in an application?

    A. Protocol analyzer

    B. Port scanner

    C. Fuzzing

    D. IPS

8. **C** is correct. Fuzzing sends random data to an application and attackers can use fuzz testers to identify vulnerabilities within applications.

A and B are incorrect. A protocol analyzer can capture and analyze IP packets and a port scanner can detect open ports, but they aren't the best choice to check vulnerabilities in an application.

D is incorrect. An organization uses an intrusion prevention system (IPS) to detect and block attacks.

Objective: 4.1 Explain the importance of application security

9. An attacker recently used a SQL injection attack against a company's web site. How can the company prevent future SQL injection attacks?

    A. Add SSL encryption

    B. Add input validation

    C. Add antivirus software

    D. Add cross-site scripting capabilities

9. **B** is correct. Input validation checks the validity of data before using it and can help prevent SQL injection, buffer overflow, and cross-site scripting attacks.

A and C are incorrect. SSL can protect confidentiality of data by encrypting it and antivirus software protects against malware such as viruses and Trojans, but neither protect against SQL injection attacks.

D is incorrect. Cross-site scripting is an attack that allows attackers to embed malicious code into a web site and you wouldn't want to enable cross-site scripting capabilities.

Objective: 4.1 Explain the importance of application security

10. Of the following choices, what could you use to deploy baseline security configurations to multiple systems?

    A. IDS

    B. Security template

    C. Change management

    D. Performance baseline

10. **B** is correct. You can use security templates to deploy baseline security configurations to multiple systems.

A is incorrect. An IDS can detect malicious activity after it occurs.

C is incorrect. A change management system helps ensure that changes don't result in unintended outages through a change, and includes the ability to document changes.

D is incorrect. A performance baseline identifies the overall performance of a system at a point in time.

Objective: 4.2 Carry out appropriate procedures to establish host security

11. An administrator wants to prevent users from installing software. Of the following choices, what is the easiest way to accomplish this?

    A. Manually remove administrative rights

    B. Implement port scanners

    C. Use a security template

    D. Implement a job rotation policy

11. **C** is correct. You can use a security template to restrict user rights and control group membership so that users don't have rights to install software.

A is incorrect. Manually removing administrative rights is possible but it requires you to touch every system and isn't as easy as using a security template.

B is incorrect. A port scanner can help determine what services and protocols are running on a remote system by identifying open ports.

D is incorrect. A job rotation policy rotates employees through different positions and can help prevent fraud.

Objective: 4.2 Carry out appropriate procedures to establish host security

12. You are troubleshooting a server that users claim is running slow. You notice that the server frequently has about 20 active SSH sessions. What can you use to determine if this is normal behavior?

    A. Vendor documentation

    B. Security template

    C. Baseline report

    D. Imaging

12. **C** is correct. Baseline reports document normal behavior of a system and you can compare current activity against the baseline report to determine what is different or abnormal.

A is incorrect. Vendor documentation identifies methods of locking down an operating system or application but won't document baseline activity.

B is incorrect. You can use security templates to deploy the same security settings to multiple systems.

D is incorrect. Images include mandated security configurations but don't show normal operation.

Objective: 4.2 Carry out appropriate procedures to establish host security

13. Your organization is considering deploying multiple servers using a standardized image. Of the following choices, what best describes the security benefit of this plan?

    A. The image can include unnecessary protocols

    B. The image provides fault tolerance as a RAID 5

    C. It eliminates Trojans

    D. The image can include mandated security configurations

13. **D** is correct. One of the benefits of an image used as a baseline is that it includes mandated security configurations to the operating system.

A is incorrect. It's common to remove unnecessary protocols on an image, not include them.

B is incorrect. RAID provides fault tolerance and increases availability for disk drives, but a standardized image is unrelated to RAID.

C is incorrect. Trojans are a type of malware that look useful to the user but are malicious.

Objective: 4.2 Carry out appropriate procedures to establish host security

14. Management is reviewing a hardware inventory in a datacenter. They realize that many of the servers are underutilized resulting in wasted resources. What can they do to improve the situation?

   A. Implement virtualization

   B. Implement VM escape

   C. Increase the datacenter footprint

   D. Add TPMs

14. **A** is correct. Virtualization can reduce the number of physical servers used by an organization, reduce the datacenter's footprint, and eliminate wasted resources.

B is incorrect. VM escape is an attack run on virtual machines allowing the attacker to access and control the physical host.

C is incorrect. Virtualization decreases the datacenter's footprint, but increasing it will result in more wasted resources.

D is incorrect. A Trusted Platform Module (TPM) is a hardware chip that stores encryption keys and provides full disk encryption, but it doesn't reduce wasted resources.

Objective: 4.2 Carry out appropriate procedures to establish host security

15. You have created an image for a database server that you plan to deploy to five physical servers. At the last minute, management decides to deploy these as virtual servers. What additional security steps do you need to take with these virtual images before deploying them?

    A. None

    B. Lock down the virtual images

    C. Install virtual antivirus software

    D. Install virtual patches

15. **A** is correct. Virtual servers have the same security requirements as physical servers so additional security steps are not required.

B and C are incorrect. The original image should include security settings and antivirus software, and should be up-to-date with current patches.

D is incorrect. Virtual servers use the same patches as physical systems and do not use virtual patches.

Objective: 4.2 Carry out appropriate procedures to establish host security

16. Of the following choices, what indicates the best method of reducing operating system vulnerabilities?

    A. Whole disk encryption

    B. Patch management

    C. Trusted Platform Module

    D. File level encryption

16. **B** is correct. Patch management is the most efficient way to combat operating system vulnerabilities.

A is incorrect. Whole disk encryption protects the confidentiality of data on a system and is useful in mobile devices, but doesn't directly reduce operating system vulnerabilities.

C is incorrect. A Trusted Platform Module supports whole disk encryption.

D is incorrect. File level encryption can prevent users, including administrators, from accessing specific files.

Objective: 4.2 Carry out appropriate procedures to establish host security

17. Of the following choices, what would you use in a patch management process?

        A. VM escape

        B. TPM

        C. Penetration testing

        D. Regression testing

17. **D** is correct. Regression testing verifies that a patch has not introduced new errors.

A is incorrect. VM escape is an attack run on a virtual machine allowing the attacker to access physical host system.

B is incorrect. A Trusted Platform Module (TPM) is a hardware chip that is included on the motherboard of many laptops, and it stores encryption keys used for full drive encryption.

C is incorrect. Penetration tests actively test security controls by attempting to exploit vulnerabilities and can cause system instability.

Objective: 4.2 Carry out appropriate procedures to establish host security

18. An organization recently suffered a significant outage due to attacks on unpatched systems. Investigation showed that administrators did not have a clear idea of when they should apply the patches. What can they do to prevent a reoccurrence of this problem?

    A. Apply all patches immediately

    B. Apply the missing patches on the attacked systems immediately

    C. Test the patches with regression testing in a test environment mirroring the production environment

    D. Create a patch management policy

18. **D** is correct. A patch management policy defines a timeline for installing patches, and can help solve this problem.

A and B are incorrect. Patches should be tested before applying them, instead of applying them immediately.

C is incorrect. It's appropriate to identify missing patches on these systems and test them with regression testing, but this only solves the immediate issue and won't prevent a reoccurrence of the problem.

Objective: 4.2 Carry out appropriate procedures to establish host security

19. Additional windows are appearing when a user surfs the Internet. These aren't malicious but the user wants them to stop. What can stop this behavior?

    A. Antivirus software

    B. Host-based firewall

    C. Pop-up blocker

    D. Input validation

19. **C** is correct. Pop-up windows are windows that appear while browsing and a pop-up blocker blocks them.

A is incorrect. Antivirus software can detect and remove many types of malware, but cannot block pop-ups.

B is incorrect. Firewalls can block intrusions but can't block pop-ups.

D is incorrect. Input validation checks input data and can help mitigate buffer overflow, SQL injection, and cross-site scripting attacks.

Objective: 4.2 Carry out appropriate procedures to establish host security

20. What type of signature-based monitoring can detect and remove known worms and Trojans?

    A. Antispyware

    B. NIDS

    C. NIPS

    D. Antivirus

20. **D** is correct. Antivirus software monitors a system and can detect and remove known malware (including worms and Trojans) based on signatures.

A is incorrect. Antispyware detects spyware, and while it can detect some types of malware, it isn't as reliable as antivirus software to detect malware.

B and C are incorrect. Intrusion detection and prevention systems do not remove malware such as worms and Trojans though they may detect network activity from a worm.

Objective: 4.2 Carry out appropriate procedures to establish host security

21. A user's computer has recently been slower than normal and has been sending out email without user interaction. Of the following choices, what is the best choice to resolve this issue?

   A. Botnet software

   B. Antispam software

   C. Anti-spyware software

   D. Antivirus software

21. **D** is correct. Antivirus software can resolve many types of malware infections and this activity indicates an infection possibly related to a botnet.

A is incorrect. Botnet software is malware that joins a computer to a botnet and does not resolve problems but causes them.

B is incorrect. Antispam software can block spam coming in but wouldn't remove malware or block emails going out.

C is incorrect. Anti-spyware software detects spyware, and some malware but isn't as good a choice as antivirus software.

Objective: 4.2 Carry out appropriate procedures to establish host security

22. What can reduce unwanted email that contains advertisements?

    A. Antispam software

    B. Antivirus software

    C. File integrity checkers

    D. Botnet software

22. **A** is correct. Antispam software can filter out unwanted or unsolicited email (also called spam).

B is incorrect. Antivirus software detects and blocks malware such as viruses, worms, and Trojans.

C is incorrect. File integrity checks can detect if a rootkit modified system files.

D is incorrect. A botnet is a network of multiple computers and attackers use them to send spam and attack other systems.

Objective: 4.2 Carry out appropriate procedures to establish host security

23. Someone stole an executive's smart phone and the phone includes sensitive data. What should you do to prevent the thief from reading the data?

    A. Password protect the phone

    B. Encrypt the data on the phone

C. Use remote wipe

D. Track the location of the phone

23. **C** is correct. Remote wipe capabilities can send a remote wipe signal to the phone to delete all the data on the phone, including any cached data.

A and B are incorrect. The phone is lost so it's too late to password protect or encrypt the data now if these steps weren't completed previously.

D is incorrect. While tracking the phone may be useful, it doesn't prevent the thief from reading the data.

Objective: 4.2 Carry out appropriate procedures to establish host security

24. What can you use to block unsolicited email?

A. Spam filter

B. Rootkit

C. Spyware

D. Antivirus software

24. **A** is correct. A spam filter filters out, or blocks, unsolicited email (spam).

B is incorrect. A rootkit is malicious software with kernel level access that hides its processes to prevent detection.

C is incorrect. Spyware is software installed on users systems without their awareness or consent.

D is incorrect. Antivirus software can detect viruses, worms, and Trojan horses.

Objective: 4.2 Carry out appropriate procedures to establish host security

25. Your organization has several portable USB drives that users are able to use to transfer large video files instead of copying them over the network. What should be used to prevent the theft of these drives when they are not being used?

    A. HSM

    B. TPM

    C. Video surveillance

    D. Locked cabinet

25. **D** is correct. A locked cabinet should be used to help prevent the theft of unused assets.

A is incorrect. A hardware security module (HSM) is used to create and store encryption keys.

B is incorrect. A Trusted Platform Module (TPM) is used for hardware encryption of entire drives.

C is incorrect. Video surveillance is useful to provide proof of someone entering or exiting a secure space, but is not needed to protect unused assets.

Objective: 4.2 Carry out appropriate procedures to establish host security

26. A company prohibits the use of USB flash drives to prevent data leakage. Of the following choices, what could the company also do to reduce data leakage?

    A. Prohibit personal music devices

    B. Remove labels from backup media

    C. Prohibit the storage of backups off-site

    D. Prohibit DLP devices

26. **A** is correct. Personal music devices use the same type of memory as USB flash drives so by prohibiting them, it can reduce data leakage.

B is incorrect. Backup media should be labeled to ensure employees recognize the value of the data.

C is incorrect. As a disaster recovery best practice, a copy of backups should be stored off-site.

D is incorrect. Network-based Data Loss Prevention (DLP) systems can examine and analyze network traffic and detect if confidential company data is included to reduce data leakage.

Objective: 4.2 Carry out appropriate procedures to establish host security

27. A file server within a network hosts files that employees throughout the company regularly access. Management wants to ensure that some personnel files on this server are not accessible by administrators. What provides the best protection?

    A. Remove administrative access to the server

    B. Protect the files with permissions

    C. Use file encryption

D. Use full disk encryption

27. **C** is correct. File level encryption is a security control that provides an additional layer of protection and can prevent administrators from accessing specific files.

A is incorrect. Administrators need access to a server to manage and maintain it so it's not feasible to remove administrative access.

B is incorrect. Permissions provide access control, but an administrator can bypass permissions.

D is incorrect. Full disk encryption is appropriate for removable storage or mobile devices, but not to protect individual files on a server.

Objective: 4.3 Explain the importance of data security

28. You organization is considering purchasing new computers that include hardware encryption capabilities. What benefit does this provide?

    A. It is faster than software encryption

    B. It does not require a TPM

    C. It does not require an HSM

    D. Reduced confidentiality

28. **A** is correct. A significant benefit of hardware encryption over software encryption is that it is faster.

B and C are incorrect. Hardware encryption methods can use a Trusted Platform Module (TPM) or a hardware security module (HSM), but the absence of either isn't a benefit of hardware encryption.

D is incorrect. Encryption helps ensure confidentiality, not reduce it.

Objective: 4.3 Explain the importance of data security

29. Your organization recently purchased several new laptop computers for employees. You're asked to encrypt the laptop's hard drives without purchasing any additional hardware. What would you use?

    A. TPM

    B. HSM

    C. VM escape

    D. DLP

29. **A** is correct. A Trusted Platform Module (TPM) is included in many new laptops, provides a mechanism for vendors to perform hard drive encryption, and does not require purchasing additional hardware.

B is incorrect. A hardware security module (HSM) is a removable hardware device and is not included with laptops, so it requires an additional purchase.

C is incorrect. A VM escape attack runs on a virtual system, and if successful, it allows the attacker to control the physical host server and all other virtual servers on the physical server.

D is incorrect. A network-based Data Loss Protection (DLP) system can examine and analyze network traffic and detect if confidential company data is included.

Objective: 4.3 Explain the importance of data security

30. Your organization is considering the purchase of new computers. A security professional stresses that these devices should include TPMs. What benefit does a TPM provide? (Choose all that apply.)

    A. It use hardware encryption, which is quicker than software encryption

    B. It use software encryption, which is quicker than hardware encryption

    C. It includes an HSM file system

    D. It stores RSA keys

30. **A** and **D** are correct. A Trusted Platform Module (TPM) is a hardware chip that stores RSA encryption keys and uses hardware encryption, which is quicker than software encryption.
B is incorrect. A TPM does not use software encryption.
C is incorrect. A hardware security module (HSM) is a removable hardware device that uses hardware encryption but it does not have a file system and TPM does not provide HSM as a benefit.
Objective: 4.3 Explain the importance of data security

31. Of the following choices, what is the best choice to provide encryption services in a clustered environment?

    A. Virtual servers

    B. SaaS provider

    C. HSM

    D. TPM

31. **C** is correct. A hardware security module (HSM) is a removable or external device that provides encryption services and can be used in a clustered environment.

A is incorrect. You may be able to configure virtual servers to provide encryption services in a clustered environment but they will not be as efficient as the hardware-based encryption provided by an HSM.

B is incorrect. A SaaS provider provides software or applications, such as webmail, via the cloud.

D is incorrect. A Trusted Platform Module (TPM) is a chip on the motherboard of a computer, and while it does provide full disk encryption services, it can't be used in a clustered environment.

Objective: 4.3 Explain the importance of data security

32. What functions does an HSM include?

    A. Reduces the risk of employees emailing confidential information outside the organization

    B. Provides webmail to clients

    C. Provides full drive encryption

    D. Generates and store keys

32. **D** is correct. A hardware security module (HSM) is a removable device that can generate and store RSA keys used for asymmetric encryption and decryption.

A is incorrect. A Data Loss Protection (DLP) device is a device that can reduce the risk of employees emailing confidential information outside the organization.

B is incorrect. A Trusted Platform Module (TPM) provides full drive encryption and is included in many laptops.

C is incorrect. SaaS provides software or applications, such as webmail, via the cloud.

Objective: 4.3 Explain the importance of data security

33. Employees regularly send email in and out of the company. The company suspects that some employees are sending out confidential data and they want to take steps to reduce this risk. What can they use?

    A. HSM

    B. TPM

    C. A network-based DLP

    D. Port scanner

33. **C** is correct. A network-based Data Loss Prevention (DLP) system can examine and analyze network traffic and detect if confidential company data is included.

A is incorrect. A hardware security module (HSM) is a removable hardware device that stores RSA keys and provides encryption services.

B is incorrect. A Trusted Platform Module (TPM) is a hardware chip that is included on the motherboard of many laptops and it stores encryption keys used for full drive encryption.

D is incorrect. A port scanner looks for open ports on a system to determine running services and protocols.

Objective: 4.3 Explain the importance of data security

34. Your organization wants to prevent losses due to data leakage on portable devices. What provides the best protection?

A. Smart cards

    B. Full disk encryption

    C. Permissions

    D. SSH

34. B is correct. Encryption, including full disk encryption, provides the best protection against data leakage on portable devices, and any data at rest.

A is incorrect. Smart cards provide authentication but won't protect data on a portable device if it falls into the wrong hands.

C is incorrect. Permissions provide access controls while a device is within a network, but an attacker can remove a portable device and bypass permissions.

D is incorrect. SSH is a good encryption protocol for data in transit, but not data at rest stored on a portable device.

Objective: 4.3 Explain the importance of data security

35. Your organization has an existing server and you want to add a hardware device to provide encryption capabilities. What is the easiest way to accomplish this?

    A. TPM

    B. HSM

    C. DLP

    D. IaaS

35. **B** is correct. A hardware security module (HSM) is a hardware device you can add to a server to provide encryption capabilities.

A is incorrect. A Trusted Platform Module (TPM) is a chip embedded into a motherboard that also provides hardware encryption, but you can't easily add a TPM to an existing server.

C is incorrect. A Data Loss Protection (DLP) device can reduce the risk of employees emailing confidential information outside the organization.

D is incorrect. Organizations use IaaS to rent access to hardware such as servers via the cloud to limit their hardware footprint and personnel costs.

Objective: 4.3 Explain the importance of data security

36. Your organization issues laptop computers to employees. Employees use them while traveling, and frequently store sensitive data on these systems. What can you use to recover a laptop if an employee loses it?

    A. Encryption

    B. Remote wipe

    C. Remote lock

    D. GPS tracking

36. **D** is correct. The goal in the question is to recover the laptop, and the only answer that helps recover it is Global Positioning System (GPS) tracking.

A is incorrect. If you wanted to protect the data before the employee lost it, full disk encryption is a good choice.

B is incorrect. If you want to erase all the data so that an attacker can't read it after the laptop is lost, you can use remote wipe.

C is incorrect. If you want to make it more difficult for an attacker to use the device, you can use remote lock to lock it with a different passcode.

Objective: 4.3 Explain the importance of data security

37. Of the following choices, what is a primary benefit of data labeling?
   A. To identify data collected from a public web site
   B. To prevent the handling of PII
   C. To identify PII
   D. Ensure that employees understand data they are handling

37. **D** is correct. Data classifications ensure that users understand the value of data and data labeling ensures that users know what data they are handling and processing.

A is incorrect. A privacy policy identifies data collected from a public web site.

B is incorrect. Personally identifiable information (PII) requires special handling, but it is not possible to prevent handling PII.

C is incorrect. Data labeling identifies all types of data and classifications, not just PII.

Objective: 4.3 Explain the importance of data security

38. A company was recently involved in a legal issue that resulted in administrators spending a significant amount of time retrieving data from archives in response to a court order. The company wants to limit the time spent on similar events in the future. What can they do?

    A. Implement separation of duties policies

    B. Implement privacy policies

    C. Create storage and retention policies

    D. Perform user rights reviews

38. **C** is correct. Storage and retention policies identify how long data is retained. They can limit a company's exposure to legal proceedings and reduce the amount of labor required to respond to court orders.

A is incorrect. A separation of duties policy separates individual tasks of an overall function between different people but doesn't affect data retention.

B is incorrect. A privacy policy identifies what data is collected from users on a web site.

D is incorrect. User rights reviews can identify violations in a user privilege policy.

Objective: 4.3 Explain the importance of data security

39. Of the following choices, what is the best way to protect the confidentiality of data?

    A. Authentication

    B. Encryption

    C. Hashing

    D. PaaS

39. **B** is correct. Encryption protects the confidentiality of data. You can encrypt any type of data including sensitive data stored on a server, a desktop, a mobile device, or within a database.

A is incorrect. Authentication proves a person's identity and is a first step in access control, but by itself, it does not provide confidentiality.

C is incorrect. Hashing ensures the integrity of data.

D is incorrect. Platform as a Service (PaaS) provides an easy to configure operating system for on-demand cloud computing.

Objective: 4.3 Explain the importance of data security

40. An organization is disposing of old hard drives. What should security personnel do to prevent data leakage?

    A. Sanitize the drive using bit level overwrites

    B. Delete all data files

    C. Format the drive

    D. Remove operating system files

40. **A** is correct. A bit level overwrite process writes a series of 1s and 0s on a drive and ensures that the disk is sanitized before disposing it.

B and C are incorrect. File deletion and drive formatting can be undone in many situations and doesn't ensure the data is removed.

D is incorrect. All files and data should be removed, not just operating system files.

Objective: 4.3 Explain the importance of data security

41. Organizations often restrict employee access of social networking sites from work locations. What are they trying to prevent?

    A. Information disclosure

    B. Employee morale

    C. Risks from DoS attacks

    D. Risks from DDoS attacks

41. **A** is correct. A risk resulting from the improper use of social networking sites is information disclosure.

B is incorrect. Some organizations allow access to various Internet sites to increase morale (not prevent it), but they provide training to users on the risks.

C and D are incorrect. Denial of service (DoS) and distributed DoS (DDoS) attacks are launched against systems, not users so accessing the social networking sites doesn't present risks of DoS or DDoS attacks.

Objective: 4.3 Explain the importance of data security

42. Which of the following is PII when it is associated with a person's full name?

    A. Pet's name

    B. Birthdate

    C. Favorite book

    D. Favorite color

42. **B** is correct. A birthdate is personally identifiable information (PII) when it is combined with a full name.

A C, and D are incorrect. These answers are not PII.

Objective: 4.3 Explain the importance of data security

43. Why would an organization use information classification practices?

   A. To enhance phishing

   B. To enhance whaling

   C. To protect sensitive data

   D. To ensure PII is publically available

43. **C** is correct. Information classification practices help protect sensitive data by ensuring that users understand the value of data. A and B are incorrect. Phishing and whaling are attacks via email. D is incorrect. Personally identifiable information (PII) requires special handling and should not be publically available.

Objective: 4.3 Explain the importance of data security

Chapter 5 Access Control and Identity Management

Access Control and Identity Management topics are **13 percent** of the CompTIA Security+ exam. The objectives in this domain are:

5.1 Explain the function and purpose of authentication services

- RADIUS
- TACACS
- TACACS+
- Kerberos
- LDAP
- XTACACS

5.2 Explain the fundamental concepts and best practices related to authentication, authorization and access control

- Identification vs. authentication
- Authentication (single factor) and authorization
- Multifactor authentication
- Biometrics
- Tokens
- Common access card
- Personal identification verification card
- Smart card
- Least privilege
- Separation of duties
- Single sign on
- ACLs
- Access control
- Mandatory access control
- Discretionary access control

- Role/rule-based access control
- Implicit deny
- Time of day restrictions
- Trusted OS
- Mandatory vacations
- Job rotation

5.3 Implement appropriate security controls when performing account management

- Mitigates issues associated with users with multiple account/roles
- Account policy enforcement
    - Password complexity
    - Expiration
    - Recovery
    - Length
    - Disablement
    - Lockout
- Group based privileges
- User assigned privileges

The CompTIA Security+: Get Certified Get Ahead SY0-301 Study Guide (ISBN 1463762364) discusses these topics in much more depth. Sec-plus.com has more details on the availability of this book.

√ **Get Certified**
    √ **Get Ahead**

Practice Test Questions for Access Control and Identity Management Domain

1. What is used for authentication in a Microsoft Active Directory domain?

    A. RADIUS

    B. TACACS+

    C. Kerberos

    D. NIDS

2. Which of the following best describes the purpose of LDAP?

    A. A central point for user management

    B. Biometric authentication

    C. Prevent loss of confidentiality

    D. Prevent loss of integrity

3. Of the following protocols, which one does not encrypt the entire authentication process, but instead, only encrypts the password in traffic between the client and server?

    A. RADIUS

    B. TACACS+

    C. XTACACS

    D. Token

4. Which one of the following AAA protocols uses multiple challenges and responses?

    A. CHAP

    B. RADIUS

    C. TACACS

    D. TACACS+

5. What is completed when a user's password has been verified?

    A. Identification

    B. Authentication

    C. Authorization

    D. Access verification

6. A user is issued a token with a number displayed in an LCD. What does this provide?

    A. Rolling password for one-time use

    B. Multifactor authentication

    C. CAC

    D. PIV

7. Which one of the following includes a photo and can be used as identification? (Choose all that apply.)

    A. CAC

    B. MAC

    C. DAC

    D. PIV

8. Which of the following is a behavioral biometric authentication model?

    A. Fingerprint

    B. Token

    C. Voice recognition

    D. Iris scan

9. Which of the following is an example of multifactor authentication?

    A. Smart card and token

    B. Smart card and PIN

    C. Thumbprint and voice recognition

    D. Password and PIN

10. Which of the following choices is an example of using multiple authentication factors?

    A. Fingerprint and retina scan

    B. Smart card and token

    C. Fingerprint and password

    D. A password and a PIN

11. Of the following choices, what provides the strongest authentication?

    A. Password

    B. Smart Card

    C. Retina scan

    D. Multifactor authentication

12. A federated user database is used to provide central authentication via a web portal. What service does this database provide?

    A. SSO

    B. Multifactor authentication

    C. CAC

    D. DAC

13. An administrator is assigning access to users in different departments based on their job functions. What access control model is the administrator using?

    A. DAC

    B. MAC

    C. RBAC

    D. CAC

14. You manage user accounts for a sales department. You have created a sales user account template to comply with the principle of least privilege. What access control model are you following?

    A. DAC

    B. MAC

    C. RBAC

    D. DACL

15. Windows systems protect files and folders with New Technology File System (NTFS). What access control model does NTFS use?

    A. Mandatory Access Control (MAC)

    B. Discretionary Access Control (DAC)

C. Rule-based Access Control (RBAC)

D. Implicit allow

16. Management wants to prevent users in the Marketing department from logging onto network systems between 6 p.m. and 5 a.m. How can this be accomplished?

    A. Use time of day restrictions

    B. Account expiration

    C. Password expiration

    D. Implement a detective control

17. Which of the following formulas represent the complexity of a password policy that requires users to use only upper and lower case letters with a length of eight characters?

    A. 52^8

    B. 26^8

    C. 8^52

    D. 8^26

18. Of the following choices, what password has a dissimilar key space than the others?

    A. Secur1tyIsFun

    B. Passw0rd

    C. ILOve$ecur1ty

    D. 4uBetutaOn

19. Robert user lets you know that he is using his username as his password since it's easier to remember. You decide to inform the user that this isn't a secure password. What explanation would you include?

    A. The password wouldn't meet account lockout requirements

    B. The password is too hard to remember

    C. The password is not long enough

    D. The password is not complex

20. Your organization has implemented a self-service password reset system. What does this provide?

    A. Password policy

    B. Certificate reset

    C. Password recovery

    D. Previous logon notification

21. A user entered the incorrect password for his account three times in a row and can no longer log on because his account is disabled. What caused this?

    A. Password policy

    B. Account disablement policy

    C. Account complexity policy

    D. Account lockout policy

22. Your organization requires users to create passwords of at least 10 characters for their user account. Which of the following is being enforced?

    A. Password length

B. Password complexity

C. Password masking

D. Password history

23. Your password policy includes a password history. What else should be configured to ensure that users aren't able to easily reuse the same password?

    A. Maximum age

    B. Minimum age

    C. Password masking

    D. Password complexity

24. Your organization has a password policy that requires employees to change their password at least every 45 days, and prevents users from reusing any of their last five passwords. However, when forced to change their password, users are changing their password five more times to keep their original password. What can resolve this security vulnerability?

    A. Modify the password policy to prevent users from changing the password until a day has passed.

    B. Modify the password policy to require users to change their password after a day has passed.

    C. Modify the password policy to remember the last 12 passwords.

    D. Modify the password policy to remember the last 24 passwords.

25. A user has forgotten his password and calls the help desk for assistance. The help desk professional will reset the password and tell the user the new password. What should the help desk professional configure to ensure the user immediately resets the password?

    A. Password masking

    B. Password complexity

    C. Password history

    D. Password expiration

26. Users in your network are required to change their passwords every 60 days. What is this an example of?

    A. Password expiration requirement

    B. Password history requirement

    C. Password length requirement

    D. Password strength requirement

27. Your company has hired a temporary contractor that needs a computer account for 60 days. You want to ensure the account is automatically disabled after 60 days. What feature would you use?

    A. Account lockout

    B. Account expiration

    C. Deletion through automated scripting

    D. Manual deletion

28. After an employee is terminated, what should be done to revoke the employee's access?

> A. Expire the password
>
> B. Lock out the account
>
> C. Delete the account
>
> D. Disable the account

29. An organization requires administrators to have two accounts. One account has administrator access and the other account is a regular user account. What can this help prevent?

> A. Whaling
>
> B. Vishing
>
> C. Escalation of privileges
>
> D. Command injection

30. An attacker is using an account from an employee that left the company three years ago. What could prevent this?

> A. Password expiration policy
>
> B. Job rotation policy
>
> C. Account expiration policy
>
> D. Separation of duties policy

Practice Test Questions with Answers for Access Control and Identity Management Domain

1. What is used for authentication in a Microsoft Active Directory domain?

    A. RADIUS

    B. TACACS+

    C. Kerberos

    D. NIDS

1. **C** is correct. Kerberos is used as a network authentication protocol in Microsoft Active Directory domains, and in UNIX realms. Kerberos uses tickets issued by a Key Distribution Center (KDC).

A and B are incorrect. RADIUS and TACACS+ are central authentication services that also provide authorization and accounting.

D is incorrect. A network-based intrusion detection service (NIDS) attempts to detect intrusions on a network.

Objective: 5.1 Explain the function and purpose of authentication services

2. Which of the following best describes the purpose of LDAP?

    A. A central point for user management

    B. Biometric authentication

    C. Prevent loss of confidentiality

D. Prevent loss of integrity

2. **A** is correct. The Lightweight Directory Access Protocol (LDAP) specifies formats and methods to query directories and is used to manage objects (such as users and computers) in an Active Directory domain.

B is incorrect. LDAP is not associated with biometrics.

C and D are incorrect. While LDAP contributes indirectly to confidentiality and integrity, it is more accurate to say that LDAP is used as a central point for user management.

Objective: 5.1 Explain the function and purpose of authentication services

3. Of the following protocols, which one does not encrypt the entire authentication process, but instead, only encrypts the password in traffic between the client and server?

    A. RADIUS

    B. TACACS+

    C. XTACACS

    D. Token

3. **A.** is correct. Remote Authentication Dial-In User Service (RADIUS) will encrypt the password packets between a client and a server, but it does not encrypt the entire authentication process.

B and C are incorrect. Terminal Access Controller Access-Control System + (TACACS+) and Extended TACACS (XTACACS) both encrypt the entire logon process.

C is incorrect. A token uses a one-time rolling password but it is not a protocol in itself.

Objective: 5.1 Explain the function and purpose of authentication services

4. Which one of the following AAA protocols uses multiple challenges and responses?

    A. CHAP

    B. RADIUS

    C. TACACS

    D. TACACS+

4. D is correct. TACACS+ uses multiple challenges and responses and is an authentication, authorization, and accounting (AAA) protocol.

A is incorrect. CHAP is not an AAA protocol.

B and C are incorrect. RADIUS and TACACS do not use multiple challenges and responses.

Objective: 5.1 Explain the function and purpose of authentication services

5. What is completed when a user's password has been verified?

    A. Identification

    B. Authentication

    C. Authorization

    D. Access verification

5. **B** is correct. A user is authenticated when the password is verified.

A is incorrect. The user claims an identity with a username.

C and D are incorrect. After authentication, users are authorized to access resources based on their identity, and auditing can verify what resources a user has accessed.

Objective: 5.2 Explain the fundamental concepts and best practices related to authentication, authorization and access control

6. A user is issued a token with a number displayed in an LCD. What does this provide?

    A. Rolling password for one-time use

    B. Multifactor authentication

    C. CAC

    D. PIV

6. A is correct. A token (such as an RSA token) provides a rolling password for one-time use.

B is incorrect. While it can be used with multifactor authentication (requiring the user to also enter other information such as a password), it doesn't provide multifactor authentication by itself.

C and D are incorrect. A CAC and a PIV are both specialized types of smart cards that include photo identification.

Objective: 5.2 Explain the fundamental concepts and best practices related to authentication, authorization and access control

7. Which one of the following includes a photo and can be used as identification? (Choose all that apply.)

    A. CAC

    B. MAC

    C. DAC

    D. PIV

7. **A** and **D** are correct. A common access card (CAC) and a personal identity verification (PIV) card both include photo identification and function as smart cards.

B and C are incorrect. MAC and DAC are access control models, not photo IDs.

Objective: 5.2 Explain the fundamental concepts and best practices related to authentication, authorization and access control

8. Which of the following is a behavioral biometric authentication model?

    A. Fingerprint

    B. Token

    C. Voice recognition

    D. Iris scan

8. **C** is correct. Voice recognition is a form of behavioral biometric authentication. Biometrics are the most difficult for an attacker to falsify or forge because they represents a user based on personal characteristics.

A and D are incorrect. Fingerprints and iris scans are forms of physical biometric authentication.

B is incorrect. A token provides a rolling password for one-time use.

Objective: 5.2 Explain the fundamental concepts and best practices related to authentication, authorization and access control

9. Which of the following is an example of multifactor authentication?

    A. Smart card and token

    B. Smart card and PIN

    C. Thumbprint and voice recognition

    D. Password and PIN

9. **B** is correct. A smart card and PIN is an example of multifactor authentication since it uses methods from the *something you have* factor and *something you know* factor.

A is incorrect. A smart card and token are both in the *something you have* factor.

C is incorrect. Thumbprint and voice recognition are both in the *something you are* factor.

D is incorrect. A password and PIN are both in the *something you know* factor.

Objective: 5.2 Explain the fundamental concepts and best practices related to authentication, authorization and access control

10. Which of the following choices is an example of using multiple authentication factors?

    A. Fingerprint and retina scan

    B. Smart card and token

    C. Fingerprint and password

    D. A password and a PIN

10. **C** is correct. A fingerprint uses the *something you are* factor, and a password uses the *something you know* factor. All the other answers use examples from the same factor.

A is incorrect. A fingerprint and retina are both examples of the *something you are* factor.

B is incorrect. A smart card and token are both examples of the *something you have* factor.

D is incorrect. A password and a PIN are both examples of the *something you know* factor.

Objective: 5.2 Explain the fundamental concepts and best practices related to authentication, authorization and access control

11. Of the following choices, what provides the strongest authentication?

    A. Password

    B. Smart Card

    C. Retina scan

    D. Multifactor authentication

11. **D** is correct. Multifactor authentication combines two or more other factors of authentication and is stronger than any authentication using a single factor.

A is incorrect. A password is *something you know.*

B is incorrect. A smart card is *something you have.*

C is incorrect. A retina scan is based on *something you are.*

Objective: 5.2 Explain the fundamental concepts and best practices related to authentication, authorization and access control

12. A federated user database is used to provide central authentication via a web portal. What service does this database provide?

    A. SSO

    B. Multifactor authentication

    C. CAC

    D. DAC

12. **A** is correct. Single sign-on (SSO) can be used to provide central authentication with a federated database and use this authentication in a non-homogeneous environment.

B is incorrect. Multifactor authentication uses authentication from two or more factors.

C is incorrect. A common access card (CAC) is a form of photo identification and also function as a smart card.

D is incorrect. DAC is an access control model.

Objective: 5.2 Explain the fundamental concepts and best practices related to authentication, authorization and access control

13. An administrator is assigning access to users in different departments based on their job functions. What access control model is the administrator using?

    A. DAC

    B. MAC

    C. RBAC

    D. CAC

13. **C** is correct. In a role based access control (RBAC) model, roles are used to define rights and permissions for users.

A is incorrect. The DAC model specifies that every object has an owner, and the owner has full explicit control of the object.

B is incorrect. The MAC model uses sensitivity labels for users and data.

D is incorrect. A CAC is an identification card that includes smart card capabilities.

Objective: 5.2 Explain the fundamental concepts and best practices related to authentication, authorization and access control

14. You manage user accounts for a sales department. You have created a sales user account template to comply with the principle of least privilege. What access control model are you following?

    A. DAC

    B. MAC

    C. RBAC

    D. DACL

14. **C** is correct. The role based access control (RBAC) model can use groups (as roles) with a user account template assigned to a group to ensure new users are granted access to only what they need and no more.

A is incorrect. The DAC model specifies that every object has an owner, and the owner has full explicit control of the object.

B is incorrect. The MAC model uses sensitivity labels for users and data.

D is incorrect. A DACL is an access control list used in the DAC model.

Objective: 5.2 Explain the fundamental concepts and best practices related to authentication, authorization and access control

15. Windows systems protect files and folders with New Technology File System (NTFS). What access control model does NTFS use?

    A. Mandatory Access Control (MAC)

    B. Discretionary Access Control (DAC)

    C. Rule-based Access Control (RBAC)

    D. Implicit allow

15. **B** is correct. Windows systems use the Discretionary Access Control (DAC) model by default for NTFS files and folders.

A is incorrect. The MAC model uses labels.

C is incorrect. Rule-based access control uses rules to determine access.

D is incorrect. There is no such access control model as implicit allow. However, implicit deny is commonly used as the last rule in a firewall to indicate that all traffic not explicitly allowed is implicitly denied.

Objective: 5.2 Explain the fundamental concepts and best practices related to authentication, authorization and access control

16. Management wants to prevent users in the Marketing department from logging onto network systems between 6 p.m. and 5 a.m. How can this be accomplished?

    A. Use time of day restrictions

    B. Account expiration

    C. Password expiration

    D. Implement a detective control

16. **A** is correct. Time of day restrictions can be used to prevent users from logging in at certain times, or even from making connections to network resources at certain times.

B is incorrect. Account expiration refers to when a temporary account is automatically disabled (such as expiring a temporary account after 60 days).

C is incorrect. Password expiration refers to the practice of setting a password to immediately expire after resetting it.

D is incorrect. A detective control won't prevent a user logging on, but can detect it after it occurred.

Objective: 5.2 Explain the fundamental concepts and best practices related to authentication, authorization and access control

17. Which of the following formulas represent the complexity of a password policy that requires users to use only upper and lower case letters with a length of eight characters?

    A. 52^8

    B. 26^8

    C. 8^{52}

    D. 8^{26}

17. **A** is correct. The correct formula is 52^8. The formula to calculate the complexity of a password is C^N, where C is the number of possible characters used, and N is the length of the password. Since both upper case (A-Z) and lower case (a-z) characters are used, C is 52, and the password has a stated length of eight characters.

B is incorrect. This would be correct if only one case was used.

C is incorrect. This indicates only eight possible characters, with a password length of 52.

D is incorrect. This indicates only eight possible characters, with a password length of 26.

Objective: 5.3 Implement appropriate security controls when performing account management

18. Of the following choices, what password has a dissimilar key space than the others?

    A. Secur1tyIsFun

    B. Passw0rd

    C. IL0ve$ecur1ty

    D. 4uBetutaOn

18. **C** is correct. IL0ve$ecur1ty has 13 characters with a mixture of all four character types (uppercase letters, lowercase letters, numbers and symbols). This has a larger key space (more possibilities) than the other passwords.

A, B, and D are incorrect. Secur1ty, Passw0rd, and 3uBetuta each use only three character types.

Objective: 5.3 Implement appropriate security controls when performing account management

19. Robert user lets you know that he is using his username as his password since it's easier to remember. You decide to inform the user that this isn't a secure password. What explanation would you include?

    A. The password wouldn't meet account lockout requirements

    B. The password is too hard to remember

    C. The password is not long enough

    D. The password is not complex

19. **D** is correct. Strong passwords do not include any part of a username, and if just the username is used, the password would not be complex.

A is incorrect. Password characteristics are not related to account lockout. Account lockout is where a user can be locked out if they enter the wrong password too many times.

B is incorrect. A username as a password would not be difficult to remember.

C is incorrect. Users with long names could have extremely long passwords so they will likely meet length requirements.

Objective: 5.3 Implement appropriate security controls when performing account management

20. Your organization has implemented a self-service password reset system. What does this provide?

    A. Password policy

    B. Certificate reset

    C. Password recovery

    D. Previous logon notification

20. **C** is correct. A self-service password reset system allows users to recover passwords without administrative intervention.

A is incorrect. A password policy ensures that users create strong passwords, and change them periodically.

B is incorrect. A password reset system does not reset certificates.

D is incorrect. A previous logon notification provides notification to users when they last logged on and can help them identify if someone else is using their account.

Objective: 5.3 Implement appropriate security controls when performing account management

21. A user entered the incorrect password for his account three times in a row and can no longer log on because his account is disabled. What caused this?

    A. Password policy

    B. Account disablement policy

    C. Account complexity policy

D. Account lockout policy

21. **D** is correct. An account lockout policy will force an account to be locked out after the wrong password is entered a set number of times (such as after three failed attempts).

A is incorrect. A password policy ensures strong passwords are used and users change their password regularly.

B is incorrect. An account disablement policy refers to disabling inactive accounts, such as after an employee is terminated.

C is incorrect. A password policy ensures users create strong, complex passwords but there is no such thing as an account complexity policy.

Objective: 5.3 Implement appropriate security controls when performing account management

22. Your organization requires users to create passwords of at least 10 characters for their user account. Which of the following is being enforced?

A. Password length

B. Password complexity

C. Password masking

D. Password history

22. **A** is correct. Requiring passwords of a specific number of characters is the password length element of a password policy.

B is incorrect. Password complexity requires the characters to be different such as upper case, lower case, numbers, and special characters.

C is incorrect. Password masking displays a special character such as *
when a user types in their password instead of showing the password in
clear text.

D is incorrect. Password history prevents users from reusing
passwords.

Objective: 5.3 Implement appropriate security controls when
performing account management

23. Your password policy includes a password history. What else
should be configured to ensure that users aren't able to easily reuse the
same password?

    A. Maximum age

    B. Minimum age

    C. Password masking

    D. Password complexity

23. **B** is correct. The minimum password age prevents users from
changing the password again until some time has passed, such as one
day.

A is incorrect. The maximum age forces a user to periodically change
their password, such as after 60 or 90 days.

C is incorrect. Password masking displays a special character such as *
when a user types in their password instead of showing the password in
clear text.

D is incorrect. Password complexity ensures the password has a
mixture of different character types and is sufficiently long.

Objective: 5.3 Implement appropriate security controls when
performing account management

24. Your organization has a password policy that requires employees to change their password at least every 45 days, and prevents users from reusing any of their last five passwords. However, when forced to change their password, users are changing their password five more times to keep their original password. What can resolve this security vulnerability?

A. Modify the password policy to prevent users from changing the password until a day has passed.

B. Modify the password policy to require users to change their password after a day has passed.

C. Modify the password policy to remember the last 12 passwords.

D. Modify the password policy to remember the last 24 passwords.

24. **A** is correct. Password policies have a minimum password age setting and if set to one day, it will prevent users from changing their password until a day has passed.

B is incorrect. Requiring users to change their password every day wouldn't resolve the problem and is not reasonable.

C is incorrect. The password history is currently set to remember the last five passwords.

D is incorrect. If you change the password history to remember the last 12 or 24 passwords, they can do the same thing described in the scenario to get back to their original password.

Objective: 5.3 Implement appropriate security controls when performing account management

25. A user has forgotten his password and calls the help desk for assistance. The help desk professional will reset the password and tell the user the new password. What should the help desk professional configure to ensure the user immediately resets the password?

    A. Password masking

    B. Password complexity

    C. Password history

    D. Password expiration

25. **D** is correct. Password expiration should be configured so that the user is forced to change the password the first time the user logs on. This ensures the help desk professional doesn't know the user's password after the user logs on.

A is incorrect. Password masking displays a special character such as * when a user types in their password instead of showing the password in clear text.

B is incorrect. Password complexity ensures the password has a mixture of different character types and is sufficiently long.

C is incorrect. Password history prevents users from reusing passwords.

Objective: 5.3 Implement appropriate security controls when performing account management

26. Users in your network are required to change their passwords every 60 days. What is this an example of?

    A. Password expiration requirement

    B. Password history requirement

C. Password length requirement

D. Password strength requirement

26. **A** is correct. A password policy can include a password expiration requirement (or a maximum age) that ensures that users change their passwords periodically, such as every 60 days or every 90 days.

B is incorrect. Password history prevents users from using previously used passwords.

C is incorrect. Password length ensures the password includes a minimum number of characters such as at least eight characters.

D is incorrect. Password strength ensures the password uses a mixture of character types.

Objective: 5.3 Implement appropriate security controls when performing account management

27. Your company has hired a temporary contractor that needs a computer account for 60 days. You want to ensure the account is automatically disabled after 60 days. What feature would you use?

A. Account lockout

B. Account expiration

C. Deletion through automated scripting

D. Manual deletion

27. **B** is correct. Most systems include a feature that allows you to set the expiration of an account when a preset deadline arrives.

A is incorrect. Account lockout locks out an account if an incorrect password is entered too many times.

C and D are incorrect. The scenario states you want to disable the account, not delete it.

Objective: 5.3 Implement appropriate security controls when performing account management

28. After an employee is terminated, what should be done to revoke the employee's access?

    A. Expire the password

    B. Lock out the account

    C. Delete the account

    D. Disable the account

28. **D** is correct. An account disablement policy would ensure that a terminated employee's account is disabled to revoke the employee's access.

A is incorrect. Expiring the password forces the user to change the password at the next logon.

B is incorrect. An account lockout policy locks out an account if an incorrect password is entered too many times.

C is incorrect. The account may be needed to access the user's resources so it is recommended to disable the account instead of deleting it.

Objective: 5.3 Implement appropriate security controls when performing account management

29. An organization requires administrators to have two accounts. One account has administrator access and the other account is a regular user account. What can this help prevent?

    A. Whaling

    B. Vishing

    C. Escalation of privileges

    D. Command injection

29. **C** is correct. Requiring administrators to use two accounts in this way helps prevent privilege escalation attacks.

A is incorrect. Whaling is a phishing attack that targets high-level executives.

B is incorrect. Vishing is a form of phishing that uses recorded voice over the telephone.

D is incorrect. A command injection attack is any attempt to inject commands into an application such as a web-based form.

Objective: 5.3 Implement appropriate security controls when performing account management

30. An attacker is using an account from an employee that left the company three years ago. What could prevent this?

    A. Password expiration policy

    B. Job rotation policy

    C. Account expiration policy

    D. Separation of duties policy

30. **C** is correct. An account disablement or account expiration policy ensures that inactive accounts are disabled.

A is incorrect. A password expiration policy requires changing the password, but wouldn't disable the account unless the user or attacker didn't change the password.

B is incorrect. Job rotation policies require employees to change roles on a regular basis but don't affect accounts.

D is incorrect. A separation of duties policy separates individual tasks of an overall function between different people.

Objective: 5.3 Implement appropriate security controls when performing account management

Chapter 6 Cryptography

Cryptography topics are **11 percent** of the CompTIA Security+ exam. The objectives in this domain are:

6.1 Summarize general cryptography concepts
- Symmetric vs. asymmetric
- Fundamental differences and encryption methods
  - o Block vs. stream
- Transport encryption
- Non-repudiation
- Hashing
- Key escrow
- Steganography
- Digital signatures
- Use of proven technologies
- Elliptic curve and quantum cryptography

6.2 Use and apply appropriate cryptographic tools and products
- WEP vs. WPA/WPA2 and preshared key
- MD5
- SHA
- RIPEMD
- AES
- DES
- 3DES
- HMAC
- RSA
- RC4
- One-time-pads
- CHAP
- PAP
- NTLM

- NTLMv2
- Blowfish
- PGP/GPG
- Whole disk encryption
- TwoFish
- Comparative strengths of algorithms
- Use of algorithms with transport encryption
  o SSL
  o TLS
  o IPSec
  o SSH
  o HTTPS

6.3 Explain the core concepts of public key infrastructure
- Certificate authorities and digital certificates
  o CA
  o CRLs
- PKI
- Recovery agent
- Public key
- Private key
- Registration
- Key escrow
- Trust models

6.4 Implement PKI, certificate management and associated components
- Certificate authorities and digital certificates
  o CA
  o CRLs
- PKI
- Recovery agent
- Public key
- Private keys

- Registration
- Key escrow
- Trust models

The CompTIA Security+: Get Certified Get Ahead SY0-301 Study Guide (ISBN 1463762364) discusses these topics in much more depth. Sec-plus.com has more details on the availability of this book.

√ **Get Certified**
   √ **Get Ahead**

Practice Test Questions for Cryptography Domain

1. What will always create a fixed size string of bits regardless of the size of the original data? (Choose all that apply.)

    A. MD5

    B. SHA

    C. One-time pad

    D. CRL

2. What are two basic components of encryption?

    A. Algorithms and keys

    B. CAs and CRLs

    C. Certificates and private keys

    D. Public keys and session keys

3. A system encrypts data prior to transmitting it over a network, and the system on the other end of the transmission media decrypts it. If the systems are using a symmetric encryption algorithm for encryption and decryption, which of the following statements are true?

    A. A symmetric encryption algorithm uses the same key to encrypt and decrypt data at both ends of the transmission media.

    B. A symmetric encryption algorithm uses different keys to encrypt and decrypt data at both ends of the transmission media.

C. A symmetric encryption algorithm does not use keys to encrypt and decrypt data at both ends of the transmission media.

D. A symmetric encryption algorithm is an insecure method used to encrypt data transmitted over transmission media.

4. Of the following choices, what is an encryption algorithm that is commonly used in small portable devices such as mobile phones?

    A. Steganography

    B. 3DES

    C. PGP

    D. Elliptic curve

5. A web site includes graphic files. A security professional is comparing the hash of a graphic file captured last week, with the hash of what appears to be the same graphic file today. What is the security professional looking for?

    A. CRL

    B. Steganography

    C. Key

    D. Digital signature

6. Which of the following protocols requires a CA for authentication?

    A. FTP

    B. PEAP-TLS

    C. AES

    D. PKI

7. An organization wants to verify the identity of anyone sending emails. The solution should also verify integrity of the emails. What can they use?

    A. AES

    B. Encryption

    C. CRL

    D. Digital signatures

8. Sally is sending an email and she encrypted a portion of the email with her private key. What can this provide?

    A. Confidentiality

    B. Validation of her certificate

    C. Non-repudiation

    D. One-time pad

9. Sally sent an encrypted email with a digital signature to Joe. Joe wants to verify the email came from Sally. How can this be achieved?

    A. Use Sally's private key to verify the digital signature

    B. Use Sally's private key to decrypt the email

    C. Use Sally's public key to verify the digital signature

    D. Use Sally's public key to decrypt the email

10. What type of key is used to sign an email message?

    A. Sender's public key

    B. Sender's private key

    C. Recipient's public key

    D. Recipient's private key

11. A system administrator wants to create a unique identifier for an executable file. Of the following choices, what can be used?

    A. RC4

    B. Public key

    C. Private key

    D. SHA

12. Of the following choices, what can ensure the integrity of email messages?

    A. MD5

    B. AES

    C. TwoFish

    D. RSA

13. Which of the following is an encryption algorithm that uses 128-bit keys?

    A. DES

    B. AES

    C. 3DES

    D. MD5

14. Which of the following uses 56-bit keys for encryption?

    A. AES

    B. DES

    C. MD5

    D. SHA

15. Which of the following is an encryption algorithm that uses multiple keys and encrypts data multiple times?

    A. DES

    B. AES

    C. 3DES

    D. MD5

16. Of the following choices, what can you use to encrypt email?

    A. HMAC

    B. RIPEMD

    C. PII

    D. S/MIME

17. Sally and Joe decide to use PGP to exchange secure email. What should Sally provide to Joe so that Joe can encrypt email before sending it to her?

    A. Her private key

    B. Her public key

    C. Her recovery key

    D. Her steganography key

18. How can a forensic analysis ensure the integrity of an image of a computer's memory?

    A. Use AES-128

    B. Use SHA-256

    C. Encrypt the image

    D. Power the system down before capturing the image

19. Which of the following statements accurately describes the relationship between keys in a PKI?

    A. Data encrypted with a public key can only be decrypted with the matching private key.

    B. Data encrypted with a public key can only be decrypted with the matching public key.

    C. Data encrypted with a private key can only be decrypted with the matching private key.

    D. The public key always encrypts and the private key always decrypts.

20. Which encryption algorithm uses prime numbers to generate keys?

    A. RSA

    B. SHA

    C. S/MIME

    D. PGP

21. Sally is sending data to Joe. She uses asymmetric encryption to encrypt the data to ensure that only Joe can decrypt it. What key does Sally use to encrypt the data?

    A. Sally's public key

    B. Sally's private key

    C. Joe's public key

    D. Joe's private key

22. A user visits an ecommerce web site and initiates a secure connection. What type of key does the web site provide to the user?

    A. Symmetric key

    B. Private key

    C. Public key

    D. MD5 key

23. Two systems need to establish a secure session between each other without any prior communication. What is needed to support this?

    A. Symmetric encryption

    B. PKI

    C. AES

    D. MD5

24. What entity verifies the authenticity of certificates?

    A. CRILL

    B. Digital signature

    C. CA

    D. Recovery agent

25. A company is using a key escrow for their PKI. What does this provide?

    A. It maintains a copy of a private key for recovery purposes

    B. It maintains a copy of a public key for recovery purposes

    C. It provides a copy of revoked certificates

    D. It provides a digital signature

26. What can a PKI recovery agent recover?

    A. Public key

    B. CRL

    C. Private key

    D. MD5 key

27. Sally encrypted a project file with her public key. Later, an administrator accidentally deleted her account that had exclusive access to her private key. Can this project file be retrieved?

    A. No. If the private key is lost, the data cannot be retrieved.

    B. Yes. The public key can decrypt the file.

    C. Yes, if a copy of her public key is stored in escrow.

    D. Yes, if the organization uses a recovery agent.

28. What includes a list of compromised or invalid certificates?

    A. CA

    B. Digital signature

    C. S/MIME

    D. CRL

29. A user browses to a web site and sees this message: "The site's certificate is not trusted." What is a likely reason?

    A. The CAs root certificate is in the trusted root certification authority store

    B. The certificate is listed in the CRL

    C. The CA is not a trusted root CA

    D. The certificate is not in the CRL

30. Which of the following choices are valid reasons to revoke a certificate holding a key? (Choose all that apply.)

    A. Key compromise

    B. CA compromise

    C. Loss of data

    D. Database breach

31. An organization wants to ensure that they do not use compromised certificates. What should they check?

    A. Trusted root certification authorities store

    B. Key escrow

    C. CRL

    D. RSA

Practice Test Questions with Answers for Cryptography Domain

1. What will always create a fixed size string of bits regardless of the size of the original data? (Choose all that apply.)

    A. MD5

    B. SHA

    C. One-time pad

    D. CRL

1. **A** and **B** are correct. Message Digest 5 (MD5) and Secure Hash Algorithm (SHA) are both hashing algorithm that create hashes of a fixed length. MD5 creates a 128-bit hash and SHA-256 creates a 256-bit hash.

C is incorrect. One-time pads are hardcopy printouts of keys in a pad of paper.

D is incorrect. A certificate revocation list (CRL) is a list of revoked certificates.

Objective: 6.1 Summarize general cryptography concepts, 6.2 Use and apply appropriate cryptographic tools and products

2. What are two basic components of encryption?

    A. Algorithms and keys

    B. CAs and CRLs

    C. Certificates and private keys

    D. Public keys and session keys

2. **A** is correct. Two basic components of encryption are algorithms and keys.

B and C are incorrect. Certificate authorities (CAs), certificates, and certificate revocation lists (CRLs) only apply to asymmetric encryption, not other types of encryption.

D is incorrect. Keys are only one element of encryption and can't encrypt data without an algorithm.

Objective: 6.1 Summarize general cryptography concepts,

3. A system encrypts data prior to transmitting it over a network, and the system on the other end of the transmission media decrypts it. If the systems are using a symmetric encryption algorithm for encryption and decryption, which of the following statements are true?

    A. A symmetric encryption algorithm uses the same key to encrypt and decrypt data at both ends of the transmission media.

    B. A symmetric encryption algorithm uses different keys to encrypt and decrypt data at both ends of the transmission media.

    C. A symmetric encryption algorithm does not use keys to encrypt and decrypt data at both ends of the transmission media.

    D. A symmetric encryption algorithm is an insecure method used to encrypt data transmitted over transmission media.

3. **A** is correct. Symmetric encryption uses the same key to encrypt and decrypt data at both ends of a transmission medium.

B is incorrect. Asymmetric encryption uses two keys for encryption and decryption.

C is incorrect. Both symmetric and asymmetric encryption use keys.

D is incorrect. Symmetric encryption is commonly used to transmit data over transmission media.

Objective: 6.1 Summarize general cryptography concepts,

4. Of the following choices, what is an encryption algorithm that is commonly used in small portable devices such as mobile phones?

    A. Steganography

    B. 3DES

    C. PGP

    D. Elliptic curve

4. **D** is correct. Elliptic curve cryptography is an encryption technology commonly used with small mobile devices and it provides strong confidentiality using the least amount of computing resources.

A is incorrect. Steganography is the practice of hiding data within a file.

B is incorrect. Triple Data Encryption Standard (3DES) is an improvement over DES and used when AES is not supported.

C is incorrect. Pretty Good Privacy (PGP) uses RSA and public key cryptography to secure email.

Objective: 6.1 Summarize general cryptography concepts

5. A web site includes graphic files. A security professional is comparing the hash of a graphic file captured last week, with the hash of what appears to be the same graphic file today. What is the security professional looking for?

    A. CRL

    B. Steganography

    C. Key

    D. Digital signature

5. **B** is correct. Steganography is the practice of hiding data within a file and comparing hashes between two apparently identical files can verify if data is hidden within a file.

A is incorrect. A certificate revocation list (CRL) is a list of revoked certificates.

C is incorrect. A key is used for encryption but a hash can't discover a key.

D is incorrect. A digital signature is an encrypted hash of a message but it wouldn't be in a graphic file.

Objective: 6.1 Summarize general cryptography concepts

6. Which of the following protocols requires a CA for authentication?

    A. FTP

    B. PEAP-TLS

    C. AES

    D. PKI

6. **B** is correct. Protected Extensible Authentication Protocol Transport Layer Security (PEAP-TLS) uses TLS for the authentication process and TLS requires a certificate provided by a certification authority (CA).

A is incorrect. File Transfer Protocol (FTP) is transferred in clear text and does not use certificates.

C is incorrect. Advanced Encryption Standard (AES) is a symmetric algorithm and doesn't use a CA.

D is incorrect. A Public Key Infrastructure (PKI) issues and manages certificates used in asymmetric encryption and verifies a certificate's authenticity.

Objective: 6.2 Use and apply appropriate cryptographic tools and products

7. An organization wants to verify the identity of anyone sending emails. The solution should also verify integrity of the emails. What can they use?

    A. AES

    B. Encryption

    C. CRL

    D. Digital signatures

7. **D** is correct. Digital signatures provide authentication (verified identification) of the sender, integrity of the message, and non-repudiation.

A and B are incorrect. Advanced Encryption Standard (AES) is a symmetric encryption algorithm that uses 128, 192, or 256-bit keys, but encryption doesn't verify identities or integrity.

C is incorrect. A certificate revocation list (CRL) is a list of revoked certificates.

Objective: 6.1 Summarize general cryptography concepts

8. Sally is sending an email and she encrypted a portion of the email with her private key. What can this provide?

    A. Confidentiality

    B. Validation of her certificate

    C. Non-repudiation

    D. One-time pad

8. **C.** is correct. A digital signature provides non-repudiation (in addition to authentication and integrity) and is encrypted with the sender's private key.

A is incorrect. Encryption provides confidentiality, but if the email is encrypted with the sender's private key, anyone with the publically available public key can decrypt it.

B is incorrect. A certification authority (CA) validates a certificate with a certificate revocation list (CRL) but the digital signature doesn't validate the certificate.

D is incorrect. A one-time pad is a hardcopy printout of encryption keys ion different pages of a pad of paper.

Objective: 6.1 Summarize general cryptography concepts

9. Sally sent an encrypted email with a digital signature to Joe. Joe wants to verify the email came from Sally. How can this be achieved?

    A. Use Sally's private key to verify the digital signature

    B. Use Sally's private key to decrypt the email

    C. Use Sally's public key to verify the digital signature

    D. Use Sally's public key to decrypt the email

9. **C.** is correct. Digital signatures provide authentication (verified identification) of the sender and are decrypted with the sender's public key (Sally's public key).

A is incorrect. Sally's private key encrypts the digital signature but it is kept private and would not be available to Joe's system.

B and D are incorrect. The sender's keys (Sally's keys) are not involved in encryption. Instead, Joe's public key would be used for encryption and Joe's private key is used for decryption, but the question asks about verification of the sender, not encryption.

Objective: 6.1 Summarize general cryptography concepts, 6.2 Use and apply appropriate cryptographic tools and products

10. What type of key is used to sign an email message?

    A. Sender's public key

    B. Sender's private key

    C. Recipient's public key

    D. Recipient's private key

10. **B** is correct. A digital signature is an encrypted hash of a message, encrypted with the sender's private key.

A is incorrect. The recipient decrypts the hash using the sender's public key.

B is incorrect.

C and D are incorrect. Recipient keys are used with encryption, but not with a digital signature.

Objective: 6.1 Summarize general cryptography concepts, 6.2 Use and apply appropriate cryptographic tools and products

11. A system administrator wants to create a unique identifier for an executable file. Of the following choices, what can be used?

    A. RC4

    B. Public key

    C. Private key

    D. SHA

11. **D is correct.** Secure Hash Algorithm (SHA) is a hashing algorithm that can ensure the integrity of data including executable files.

A is incorrect. RC4 is an encryption algorithm, not a hashing algorithm.

B and C are incorrect. Public and private keys are used in asymmetric encryption.

Objective: 6.1 Summarize general cryptography concepts, 6.2 Use and apply appropriate cryptographic tools and products

12. Of the following choices, what can ensure the integrity of email messages?

    A. MD5

    B. AES

    C. TwoFish

    D. RSA

12. **A** is correct. Message Digest 5 (MD5) is a hashing algorithm that can ensure the integrity of data including email messages.

B and C are incorrect. Advanced Encryption Standard (AES) and TwoFish are symmetric encryption algorithms, not hashing algorithms.

D is incorrect. RSA is an asymmetric encryption algorithm based on prime numbers.

Objective: 6.2 Use and apply appropriate cryptographic tools and products

13. Which of the following is an encryption algorithm that uses 128-bit keys?

    A. DES

    B. AES

    C. 3DES

    D. MD5

13. **B** is correct. Advanced Encryption Standard (AES) uses 128, 192, or 256-bit keys.

A is incorrect. Data Encryption Standard (DES) uses 56-bit keys.

C is incorrect. 3DES uses 56, 112, or 168-bit keys.

D is incorrect. MD5 is a hashing algorithm used to enforce integrity.

Objective: 6.2 Use and apply appropriate cryptographic tools and products

14. Which of the following uses 56-bit keys for encryption?

    A. AES

    B. DES

    C. MD5

    D. SHA

14. **B is correct.** Data Encryption Standard (DES) uses 56-bit keys and is a weak encryption protocol.

A is incorrect. Advanced Encryption Standard (AES) uses 128, 192, or 256-bit keys.

C and D are incorrect. MD5 and SHA are hashing algorithms, but the question is asking about encryption.

Objective: 6.2 Use and apply appropriate cryptographic tools and products

15. Which of the following is an encryption algorithm that uses multiple keys and encrypts data multiple times?

    A. DES

    B. AES

    C. 3DES

    D. MD5

15. **C is correct.** Triple Data Encryption Standard (3DES) is an improvement over DES and encrypts data using multiple keys and multiple passes of the DES algorithm.

A is incorrect. Data Encryption Standard (DES) uses a single 56-bit key and encrypts the data one time.

B is incorrect. Advanced Encryption Standard (AES) use a single 128-bit, 192-bit, or 256-bit key, and is preferable over 3DES. However, if hardware doesn't support AES, 3DES may be used.

D is incorrect. MD5 is a hashing algorithm used to enforce integrity.

Objective: 6.2 Use and apply appropriate cryptographic tools and products

16. Of the following choices, what can you use to encrypt email?

    A. HMAC

    B. RIPEMD

    C. PII

    D. S/MIME

16. **D is correct.** Secure/Multipurpose Internet Mail Extensions (S/MIME) can encrypt email at rest (stored on a drive) and in transit (sent over the network).

A and B are incorrect. Hash-based Message Authentication Code (HMAC) and RACE Integrity Primitives Evaluation Message Digest (RIPEMD) are both hashing algorithms used to provide integrity.

C is incorrect. Pretty Good Privacy (PGP) can also encrypt email, but personally identifiable information cannot encrypt or decrypt data.

Objective: 6.2 Use and apply appropriate cryptographic tools and products

17. Sally and Joe decide to use PGP to exchange secure email. What should Sally provide to Joe so that Joe can encrypt email before sending it to her?

    A. Her private key

    B. Her public key

    C. Her recovery key

    D. Her steganography key

17. **B** is correct. Pretty Good Privacy (PGP) uses RSA and public key cryptography and email is encrypted with the recipient's public key (Sally's public key).

A is incorrect. Users will never give out their private key.

C is incorrect. A recovery key is used to recover encrypted data if the user's private key is inaccessible.

D is incorrect. Steganography doesn't use a key.

Objective: 6.2 Use and apply appropriate cryptographic tools and products

18. How can a forensic analysis ensure the integrity of an image of a computer's memory?

    A. Use AES-128

    B. Use SHA-256

    C. Encrypt the image

    D. Power the system down before capturing the image

18. **B** is correct. You can ensure integrity with hashing algorithms such as SHA-256, and this includes images of memory and images of disks.

A and C are incorrect. Advanced Encryption Standard 128 (AES-128) is an encryption algorithm that uses 128 bits but encryption helps ensure confidentiality, not integrity.

D is incorrect. Information in memory is lost if the system is powered down.

Objective: 6.2 Use and apply appropriate cryptographic tools and products

19. Which of the following statements accurately describes the relationship between keys in a PKI?

    A. Data encrypted with a public key can only be decrypted with the matching private key.

    B. Data encrypted with a public key can only be decrypted with the matching public key.

    C. Data encrypted with a private key can only be decrypted with the matching private key.

    D. The public key always encrypts and the private key always decrypts.

19. **A** is correct. Data encrypted with a public key can only be decrypted with the matching private key, and data encrypted with the private key can only be encrypted with the matching public key.

B is incorrect. The same asymmetric key used to encrypt data cannot decrypt the same data.

C and D are incorrect. Depending on the usage, either the public key or the private key can encrypt or decrypt.

Objective: 6.3 Explain the core concepts of public key infrastructure

20. Which encryption algorithm uses prime numbers to generate keys?

    A. RSA

    B. SHA

    C. S/MIME

    D. PGP

20. **A** is correct. RSA uses prime numbers to generate public and private keys.

B is incorrect. Secure Hash Algorithm (SHA) is a hashing algorithm that can ensure the integrity of data and it doesn't use a key.

C and D are incorrect. S/MIME and PGP digitally sign and encrypt email, and both use RSA, but they don't generate keys with prime numbers.

Objective: 6.3 Explain the core concepts of public key infrastructure

21. Sally is sending data to Joe. She uses asymmetric encryption to encrypt the data to ensure that only Joe can decrypt it. What key does Sally use to encrypt the data?

    A. Sally's public key

    B. Sally's private key

    C. Joe's public key

    D. Joe's private key

21. **C** is correct. Sally uses Joe's public key (the recipient's public key) to encrypt the data. Because Joe is the only person with Joe's private key, Joe is the only person that can decrypt the data.

A and B are incorrect. Sally would use her private key to create a digital signature, but would not use her keys for encryption.

D is incorrect. Sally would not have access to Joe's private key.

Objective: 6.3 Explain the core concepts of public key infrastructure

22. A user visits an ecommerce web site and initiates a secure connection. What type of key does the web site provide to the user?

    A. Symmetric key

    B. Private key

    C. Public key

    D. MD5 key

22. **C** is correct. The web site provides its public key in a certificate and the user's system uses this to encrypt a symmetric key.

A is incorrect. The symmetric key encrypts data in the session.

B is incorrect. Private keys are kept private so the web site will not provide their private key to the user.

D is incorrect. Message Digest 5 (MD5) is a hashing algorithm that can ensure the integrity of data but it doesn't use a key.

Objective: 6.3 Explain the core concepts of public key infrastructure

23. Two systems need to establish a secure session between each other without any prior communication. What is needed to support this?

    A. Symmetric encryption

    B. PKI

    C. AES

    D. MD5

23. **B** is correct. A Public Key Infrastructure (PKI) is a group of technologies used to request, create, manage, store, distribute, and revoke digital certificates used with asymmetric encryption.

A is incorrect. Asymmetric encryption, not symmetric encryption, allows two entities to privately share symmetric keys without any prior communication.

C is incorrect. Advanced Encryption Standard (AES) is a symmetric encryption algorithm that uses 128, 192, or 256-bit keys.

D is incorrect. Message Digest 5 (MD5) is a hashing algorithm that can ensure the integrity of data.

Objective: 6.3 Explain the core concepts of public key infrastructure

24. What entity verifies the authenticity of certificates?

    A. CRILL

    B. Digital signature

    C. CA

    D. Recovery agent

24. **C** is correct. A certificate authority (CA) within a public key infrastructure (PKI) verifies authenticity of certificates.

A is incorrect. The certificate revocation list (CRL not CRILL) includes a list of revoked certificates and is published by the CA.

B is incorrect. Digital signatures provide authentication (verified identification) of the sender, integrity, and non-repudiation for email.

D is incorrect. A recovery agent can recover an encryption key or encrypted data if the original key is lost.

Objective: 6.3 Explain the core concepts of public key infrastructure

25. A company is using a key escrow for their PKI. What does this provide?

    A. It maintains a copy of a private key for recovery purposes

    B. It maintains a copy of a public key for recovery purposes

    C. It provides a copy of revoked certificates

    D. It provides a digital signature

25 **A.** is correct. A key escrow stores a copy of private keys used within a public key infrastructure (PKI) that can be used if the original private key is lost or inaccessible.

B is incorrect. Public keys are publically available and do not need to be stored in escrow.

C is incorrect. Revoked certificates are identified in a certificate revocation list (CRL) and there's no need to keep a copy of revoked certificates.

D is incorrect. Digital signatures provide authentication (verified identification) of the sender, integrity of the message, and non-repudiation for email.

Objective: 6.3 Explain the core concepts of public key infrastructure

26. What can a PKI recovery agent recover?

    A. Public key

    B. CRL

    C. Private key

    D. MD5 key

26. **C** is correct. Public Key Infrastructure (PKI) recovery agents can recover private keys, or in some cases recover encrypted data using a different key.

A is incorrect. Public keys are public and do not need to be recovered.

B is incorrect. A certification revocation list (CRL) is a publically available list of revoked certificates.

D is incorrect. Message Digest 5 (MD5) is a hashing algorithm that can ensure the integrity of data but it does not use a key.

Objective: 6.3 Explain the core concepts of public key infrastructure

27. Sally encrypted a project file with her public key. Later, an administrator accidentally deleted her account that had exclusive access to her private key. Can this project file be retrieved?

    A. No. If the private key is lost, the data cannot be retrieved.

    B. Yes. The public key can decrypt the file.

    C. Yes, if a copy of her public key is stored in escrow.

    D. Yes, if the organization uses a recovery agent.

27. D is correct. If an organization uses a recovery agent, the recovery agent can decrypt the file, in some cases by recovering a copy of the private key, and in other cases by using a special recovery agent key.

A and B are incorrect. Data encrypted with a public key cannot be decrypted with the same public key.

C is incorrect. A private key is stored in escrow, but a public key would not be stored in escrow.

Objective: 6.3 Explain the core concepts of public key infrastructure

28. What includes a list of compromised or invalid certificates?

    A. CA

    B. Digital signature

    C. S/MIME

    D. CRL

28. D is correct. A certificate revocation list (CRL) is a list of revoked certificates and certificates are revoked if they are compromised or invalid.

A is incorrect. A certificate authority (CA) publishes the CRL making it publically available.

B is incorrect. Digital signatures provide authentication (verified identification) of the sender, integrity of the message, and non-repudiation.

C is incorrect. Secure/Multipurpose Internet Mail Extensions (S/MIME) secures email with encryption and digital signatures.

Objective: 6.3 Explain the core concepts of public key infrastructure

29. A user browses to a web site and sees this message: "The site's certificate is not trusted." What is a likely reason?

    A. The CAs root certificate is in the trusted root certification authority store

    B. The certificate is listed in the CRL

    C. The CA is not a trusted root CA

    D. The certificate is not in the CRL

29. **C** is correct. If the certificate authority (CA) isn't trusted, web browsers will display a message indicating that the site's certificate is not trusted.

A is incorrect. If the CAs root certificate is in the trusted root certification store, the certificate will be trusted.

B is incorrect. If a certificate is in the certification revocation list (CRL), the browser will indicate the certificate is revoked, but it won't indicate a lack of trust.

D is incorrect. If it's not in the CRL, it indicates it is not revoked.

Objective: 6.4 Implement PKI, certificate management and associated components

30. Which of the following choices are valid reasons to revoke a certificate holding a key? (Choose all that apply.)

    A. Key compromise

    B. CA compromise

    C. Loss of data

    D. Database breach

30. **A** and **B** are correct. Valid reasons to revoke a certificate include key compromise and CA compromise.

C and D are incorrect. A certificate is not revoked in response to loss of data or a database breach unless this actually compromised the key or the CA.

Objective: 6.4 Implement PKI, certificate management and associated components

31. An organization wants to ensure that they do not use compromised certificates. What should they check?

    A. Trusted root certification authorities store

    B. Key escrow

    C. CRL

    D. RSA

31. **C** is correct. A certificate revocation list (CRL) is a list of revoked certificates and regularly retrieving a copy of the CRL to validate certificates reduces the risk of using compromised certificates.

A is incorrect. The trusted root certification authorities store identifies trusted certificate authorities (CAs).

B is incorrect. A key escrow stores a copy of private keys used within a public key infrastructure (PKI) for recovery purposes.

D is incorrect. RSA is a public key encryption method based on prime numbers.

Objective: 6.4 Implement PKI, certificate management and associated components

Acronym List

This acronym list provides you with a quick reminder of many of the different Security+ related terms along with a short explanation. These concepts are explained in greater depth in the full version of the CompTIA Security+ Get Certified Get Ahead: SY0-301 Study Guide.

802.1x – A port based authentication protocol. Wireless can use 802.1X. For example, WPA2-Enterprise mode uses an 802.1X server (implemented as a RADIUS server) to add authentication.

3DES – Triple Digital Encryption Standard. A symmetric algorithm used to encrypt data and provide confidentiality. It was originally designed as a replacement for DES. It uses multiple keys and multiple passes and is not as efficient as AES, but is still used in some applications, such as when hardware doesn't support AES.

AAA – Authentication, Authorization, and Accounting. AAA protocols are used in remote access systems. For example, TACACS+ is an AAA protocol that uses multiple challenges and responses during a session. Authentication verifies a user's identification. Authorization determines if they should have access. Accounting tracks their access with logs.

ACE – Access Control Entry. Identifies a user or group that is granted permission to a resource. ACEs are contained within a DACL in NTFS.

ACL – Access control list. A list of rules used to grant access to a resource. In NTFS, a list of ACEs makes up the ACL for a resource. In a firewall, an ACL identifies traffic that is allowed or blocked based on IP addresses, networks, ports, and some protocols (using the protocol ID).

AES – Advanced Encryption Standard. A symmetric algorithm used to encrypt data and provide confidentiality. AES is quick, highly secure, and used in a wide assortment of cryptography schemes. It includes key sizes of 128-bits, 192-bits, or 256-bits.

AES256 – Advanced Encryption Standard 256-bit. AES sometimes includes the number of bits used in the encryption keys and AES256 uses 256-bit encryption keys.

AH – Authentication Header. IPsec includes both AH and ESP. AH provides authentication and integrity, and ESP provides confidentiality, integrity, and authentication. AH is identified with protocol ID number 51.

ALE – Annualized loss expectancy. Used to measure risk with annualized rate of occurrence (ARO) and single loss expectancy (SLE). The ALE identifies the total amount of loss expected for a given risk. The calculation is SLE * ARO = ALE.

AP – Access point, short for wireless access point (WAP). APs provide access to a wired network to wireless clients. Many APs support isolation mode to segment wireless uses from other wireless users.

ARO – Annualized rate of occurrence. Used to measure risk with annualized loss expectancy (ALE) and single loss expectancy (SLE). The ARO identifies how many times a loss is expected to occur in a year. The calculation is SLE * ARO = ALE.

ARP – Address Resolution Protocol. Resolves IP addresses to MAC addresses. ARP poisoning attacks can redirect traffic through an attacker's system by sending false MAC address updates. VLAN segregation helps prevent the scope of ARP poisoning attacks within a network.

AUP – Acceptable use policy. An AUP defines proper system usage. It will often describe the purpose of computer systems and networks, how users can access them, and the responsibilities of users when accessing the systems.

BCP – Business continuity plan. A plan that helps an organization predict and plan for potential outages of critical services or functions. It includes disaster recovery elements that provide the steps used to return critical functions to operation after an outage. A BIA is a part of a BCP and the BIA drives decisions to create redundancies such as failover clusters or alternate sites.

BIA – Business impact analysis. The BIA identifies critical business or mission requirements and includes elements such as Recovery Time Objectives (RTOs) and Recovery Point Objectives (RPOs), but it doesn't identify solutions.

BIOS – Basic Input/Output System. A computer's firmware used to manipulate different settings such as the date and time, boot drive, and access password.

BOTS – Network Robots. An automated program or system used to perform one or more tasks.

A malicious botnet is group of computers called zombies controlled through a command and control server. Attackers use malware to join computers to botnets. Zombies regularly check in with the command and control server and can launch DDoS attacks against other victims. Botnet activity often includes hundreds of outbound connections and some botnets use Internet Relay Chat (IRC) channels.

CA – Certificate Authority. An organization that manages, issues, and signs certificates and is part of a PKI. Certificates are an important part of asymmetric encryption. Certificates include public keys along with details on the owner of the certificate and on the CA that issued the certificate. Certificate owners share their public key by sharing a copy of their certificate.

CAC – Common Access Card. A specialized type of smart card used by United States Department of Defense. It includes photo identification and provides confidentiality, integrity, authentication, and non-repudiation for the users. It is similar to a PIV.

CAN – Controller Area Network. A standard that allows microcontrollers and devices to communicate with each other without a host computer.

CCMP – Counter Mode with Cipher Block Chaining Message Authentication Code Protocol. An encryption protocol based on AES used with WPA2 for wireless security. Is it is more secure then TKIP used with the original release of WPA.

CCTV – Closed-circuit television. This is a detective control that provides video surveillance. Video surveillance provides reliable proof of a person's location and activity. It can be used by an organization to verify if any equipment or data is being removed.

CERT – Computer Emergency Response Team. A group of experts that respond to security incidents. Also known as CIRT, SIRT, or IRT.

CHAP – Challenge Handshake Authentication Protocol. Authentication mechanism where a server challenges a client. MS-CHAPv2 is an improvement over CHAP and uses mutual authentication.

CIA – Confidentiality, integrity, and availability. These three form the security triad. Confidentiality helps prevent the unauthorized disclosure of data. Integrity provides assurances that data has not been modified, tampered with, or corrupted. Availability indicates that data and services are available when needed.

CIRT – Computer Incident Response Team. A group of experts that respond to security incidents. Also known as CERT, SIRT, or IRT.

COOP – Continuity of Operations Plan. A COOP site provides an alternate location for operations after a critical outage. A hot site includes personnel, equipment, software, and communications capabilities of the primary site with all the data up-to-date. A hot site can take over for a failed primary site within an hour. A cold site will have power and connectivity needed for COOP activation, but little else. A warm site is a compromise between a hot site and a cold site.

CRC – Cyclical Redundancy Check. An error detection code used to detect accidental changes that can affect the integrity of data.

CRL – Certification Revocation List. A list of certificates that have been revoked. Certificates are commonly revoked if they are compromised. The certificate authority (CA) that issued the certificate publishes a CRL and a CRL is public.

DAC – Discretionary Access Control. An access control model where all objects have owners and owners can modify permissions for the objects (files and folders). Microsoft's NTFS uses the DAC model. Other access control models are MAC and RBAC.

DACL – Discretionary Access Control List. List of Access Control Entries (ACEs) in Microsoft's NTFS. Each ACE includes a security identifier (SID) and a permission.

DDoS – Distributed denial-of-service. An attack on a system launched from multiple sources intended to make a computer's resources or services unavailable to users. DDoS attacks are often launched from zombies in botnets. DDoS attacks typically include sustained, abnormally high network traffic. A performance baseline helps administrators detect a DDoS. Compare to DoS.

DEP – Data Execution Prevention. A security feature in some operating systems. It helps prevent an application or service from executing code from a non-executable memory region

DES – Digital Encryption Standard. An older symmetric encryption standard used to provide confidentiality. DES uses 56 bits and is considered cracked.

DHCP – Dynamic Host Configuration Protocol. A service used to dynamically assign TCP/IP configuration information to clients. DHCP is often used to assign IP addresses, subnet masks, default gateways, DNS server addresses, and much more.

DLL – Dynamic Link Library. A compiled set of code that can be called from other programs.

DLP – Data Loss Protection. A network-based DLP system can examine and analyze network traffic. It can detect if confidential company data or any PII data is included in email, and reduce the risk of internal users emailing sensitive data outside the organization.

DMZ – Demilitarized zone. Area between two firewalls separating the Internet and an internal network. A DMZ provides a layer of protection for Internet-facing servers. It allows access to a server or service for Internet users while segmenting and protecting access to the internal network.

DNS – Domain Name System. Used to resolve host names to IP addresses. DNS is the primary name resolution service used on the Internet and is also used on internal networks. DNS uses port 53. DNS poisoning attempts to modify or corrupt cached DNS results. A pharming attack is a specific type of DNS poisoning attack that redirects a website's traffic to another website.

DoS – Denial-of-service. An attack from a single source that attempts to disrupt the services provided by another system. Examples include SYN Flood, smurf, and some buffer overflow attacks. Compare to DDoS.

DRP – Disaster recovery plan. A document designed to help a company respond to disasters, such as hurricanes, floods, and fires. It includes a hierarchical list of critical systems, and often prioritizes services to restore after an outage. Testing validates the plan. Recovered systems are tested before returning them to operation and this can include a comparison to baselines. The final phase of disaster recovery includes a review to identify any lessons learned and may include an update of the plan.

DSA – Digital Signature Algorithm. A digital signature is an encrypted hash of a message. The sender's private key encrypts the hash of the message to create the digital signature. The recipient decrypts the hash with the sender's public key, and if successful, it provides authentication, non-repudiation, and integrity. Authentication identifies the sender. Integrity verifies the message has not been modified. Non-repudiation is used with online transactions and prevents the sender from later denying they sent the email.

EAP – Extensible Authentication Protocol. An authentication framework that provides general guidance for authentication methods. Variations include LEAP and PEAP

ECC – Elliptic curve cryptography. An asymmetric encryption algorithm commonly used with smaller wireless devices. It uses smaller key sizes and requires less processing power than many other encryption methods

EFS – Encrypting File System. A feature within NTFS on Windows systems that supports encrypting individual files or folders for confidentiality.

EMI – Electromagnetic interference. Interference caused by motors, power lines, and fluorescent lights. Cables can be shielded to protect signals from EMI. Additionally, EMI shielding prevents signal emanation, so it can prevent someone from capturing network traffic.

ESP – Encapsulating Security Protocol. IPsec includes both AH and ESP. AH provides authentication and integrity, and ESP provides confidentiality, integrity, and authentication. ESP is identified with protocol ID number 50.

FTP – File Transfer Protocol. Used to upload and download files to an FTP server. FTP uses ports 20 and 21. Secure FTP (SFTP) uses SSH for encryption on port 22. FTP Secure (FTPS) uses SSL or TLS for encryption.

FTPS – File Transfer Protocol Secure. An extension of FTP that uses SSL or TLS to encrypt FTP traffic. Some implementations of FTPS use ports 989 and 990.

GPG – GNU Privacy Guard (GPG). Free software that is based on the OpenPGP standard. It is similar to PGP, but avoids any conflict with existing licensing by using open standards.

GPO – Group Policy object. Group Policy is used within Microsoft Windows to manage users and computers. It is implemented on a domain controller within a domain. Administrators use it to create password policies, lock down the GUI, configure host-based firewalls, and much more.

GPS – Global Positioning System. GPS tracking can help locate lost mobile devices. Remote wipe, or remote sanitize, erases all data on lost devices. Full disk encryption protects the data on the device if it is lost.

GRE - Generic Routing Encapsulation. A tunneling protocol developed by Cisco Systems.

GUI – Graphical user interface. Users interact with the graphical elements instead of typing in commands from a text interface. Windows is an example of a GUI.

HDD – Hard disk drive. A disk drive that has one or more platters and a spindle. In contrast, USB flash drives use flash memory.

HIDS – Host-based intrusion detection system. An IDS used to monitor an individual server or workstation. It protects local resources on the host such as the operating system files.

HIPS – Host-Based Intrusion Prevention System. An extension of a host-based IDS. Designed to react in real time to catch an attack in action.

HMAC – Hash-based Message authentication code. An HMAC is a fixed length string of bits similar to other hashing algorithms such as MD5 and SHA-1, but it also uses a secret key to add some randomness to the result.

HSM – Hardware security module. A removable or external device that can generate, store, and manage RSA keys used in asymmetric encryption. High-volume ecommerce sites use HSMs to increase the performance of SSL sessions. High-availability clusters needing encryption services can use clustered HSMs.

HTML – HyperText Markup Language. Language used to create web pages served on the Internet. HTML documents are displayed by web browsers and delivered over the Internet using HTTP or HTTPS. It uses less than and greater than characters (< and > to create tags. Many sites use input validation to block these tags and prevent cross-site scripting attacks.

HTTP – Hypertext Transfer Protocol. Used for web traffic on the Internet and in intranets. HTTP uses port 80.

HTTPS – Hypertext Transfer Protocol Secure. Encrypts HTTP traffic with SSL or TLS using port 443.

HVAC – Heating, ventilation, and air conditioning. HVAC systems increase availability by regulating airflow within datacenters and server rooms. They use hot and cold to regulate the cooling, thermostats to ensure a relatively constant temperature, and humidity controls to reduce the potential for static discharges, and damage from condensation. They are often integrated with fire alarm systems and either have dampers or the ability to be turned off in the event of a fire.

IaaS –Infrastructure as a Service. A cloud computing technology useful for heavily utilized systems and networks. Organizations can limit their hardware footprint and personnel costs by renting access to hardware such as servers. Compare to PaaS and SaaS.

ICMP – Internet Control Message Protocol. Used for diagnostics such as ping. Many DoS attacks use ICMP. It is common to block ICMP at firewalls and routers. If ping fails, but other connectivity to a server succeeds, it indicates that ICMP is blocked.

ID – Identification. For example, a protocol ID identifies a protocol based on a number. AH is identified with protocol ID number 51 and ESP is identified with protocol ID number 50.

IDS – Intrusion detection system. A detective control used to detect attacks after they occur. A signature-based IDS (also called definition-based) uses a database of predefined traffic patterns. An anomaly-based IDS (also called behavior-based) starts with a performance baseline of normal behavior and compares network traffic against this baseline. An IDS can be either host-based (HIDS) or network-based (NIDS). In contrast, a firewall is a preventative control that attempts to prevent the attacks before they occur. An IPS is a preventative control that will stop an attack in progress.

IEEE – Institute of Electrical and Electronic Engineers. International organization with a focus on electrical, electronics, and information technology topics. IEEE standards are well respected and followed by vendors around the world.

IGMP – Internet Group Management Protocol. Used for multicasting. Computers belonging to a multicasting group have a multicasting IP address in addition to a standard unicast IP address.

IIS – Internet Information Services. A Microsoft Windows web server. IIS comes free with Microsoft Windows Server products.

IKE – Internet Key Exchange. Used with IPsec to create a secure channel over port 500 in a VPN tunnel.

IM – Instant Messaging. Real-time direct text-based communication between two or more people, often referred to as chat.

IMAP4 – Internet Message Access Protocol v4. Used to store email on servers and allow clients to manage their email on the server. IMAP4 uses port 143.

IPS – Intrusion prevention system. A preventative control that will stop an attack in progress. It is similar to an active IDS except that it's placed in line with traffic. An IPS can actively monitor data streams, detect malicious content, and stop attacks in progress.

IPsec – Internet Protocol Security. Used to encrypt traffic on the wire and can operate in both tunnel mode and transport mode. It uses tunnel mode for VPN traffic. IPsec is built into IPv6, but can also work with IPv4 and it includes both AH and ESP. AH provides authentication and integrity, and ESP provides confidentiality, integrity, and authentication. IPsec uses port 500 for IKE with VPN connections.

IPv4 – Internet Protocol version 4. Identifies hosts using a 32-bit IP address. IPv4 is expressed in dotted decimal format with decimal numbers separated by dots or periods like this: 192.168.1.1.

IPv6 – Internet Protocol version 6. Identifies hosts using a 128-bit address. IPv6 is expressed as eight groups of four hexadecimal characters (numbers and letters), such as this: FE80: 0000:0000:0000: 20D4:3FF7:003F:DE62.

IRC – Internet Relay Chat. A form of real-time Internet text messaging often used with chat sessions. Some botnets have used IRC channels to control zombie computers through a command and control server.

IRT– Incident Response Team. A group of experts that respond to security incidents. Also known as CERT, CIRT, or SIRT.

ISP – Internet Service Provider. Company that provides Internet access to customers.

IV - Initialization vector. An provides randomization of encryption keys to help ensure that keys are not reused. WEP was susceptible to IV attacks because it used relatively small IVs. In an IV attack, the attacker uses packet injection, increasing the number of packets to analyze, and discovers the encryption key.

KDC – Key Distribution Center. Part of the Kerberos protocol used for network authentication. The KDC issues time-stamped tickets that expire.

L2TP – Layer 2 Tunneling Protocol. Tunneling protocol used with VPNs. L2TP is commonly used with IPsec (L2TP/IPsec). L2TP uses port 1701.

LAN – Local area network. Group of hosts connected within a network.

LANMAN – Local Area Network Manager. Older authentication protocol used to provide backward compatibility to Windows 9x clients. LANMAN passwords are easily cracked due to how they are stored.

LDAP – Lightweight Directory Access Protocol. Language used to communicate with directories such as Microsoft's Active Directory. It provides a central location to manage user accounts and other directory objects. LDAP uses port 389 when unencrypted and port 636 when encrypted.

LEAP – Lightweight Extensible Authentication Protocol. A modified version of the Challenge Handshake Authentication Protocol (CHAP) created by Cisco.

MAC – Mandatory Access Control. Access control model that uses sensitivity labels assigned to objects (files and folders) and subjects (users). SELinux (deployed in both Linux and UNIX platforms) is a trusted operating system platform using the MAC model. Other access control models are DAC and RBAC.

MAC – Media access control. A 48-bit address used to uniquely identify network interface cards. It also called a hardware address or a physical address, and is commonly displayed as six pairs of hexadecimal characters. Port security on a switch can limit access using MAC filtering. Wireless access points can use MAC filtering to restrict access to only certain clients, though an attacker can easily beat this.

MAC – Message authentication code. Method used to provide integrity for messages. A MAC uses a secret key to encrypt the hash. Some versions called HMAC.

MAN – Metropolitan Area Network. A computer network that spans a metropolitan area such as a city or a large campus

MBR – Master Boot Record. An area on a hard disk in its first sector. When the BIOS boots a system, it looks at the MBR for instructions and information on how to boot the disk and load the operating system. Some malware tries to hide here.

MD5 – Message Digest 5. A hashing function used to provide integrity. MD5 uses 128 bits. A hash is simply a number created by applying the algorithm to a file or message at different times. The hashes are compared to each other to verify that integrity has been maintained.

MITM – Man-in-the-middle. A MITM attack is a form of active interception allowing an attacker to intercept traffic and insert malicious code sent to other clients. Kerberos provides mutual authentication and helps prevent MITM attacks.

MS-CHAP – Microsoft Challenge Handshake Authentication Protocol. Microsoft's implementation of CHAP. MS-CHAPv2 provides mutual authentication.

MTU – Maximum Transmission Unit. The MTU identifies the size of data that can be transferred.

NAC – Network access control. Inspects clients for health and can restrict network access to unhealthy clients to a remediation network. Clients run agents and these agents report status to a NAC server. NAC is used for VPN and internal clients. MAC filtering is a form of NAC.

NAT – Network Address Translation. A service that translates public IP addresses to private and private IP addresses to public. It hides addresses on an internal network.

NIDS – Network-based intrusion detection system. IDS used to monitor a network. It can detect network-based attacks, such as smurf attacks. A NIDS cannot monitor encrypted traffic, and cannot monitor traffic on individual hosts.

NIPS – Network-Based Intrusion Prevention System. An IPS that monitors the network. An IPS can actively monitor data streams, detect malicious content, and stop attacks in progress.

NIST – National Institute of Standards and Technology. NIST is a part of the U.S. Department of Commerce and it includes an Information Technology Laboratory (ITL). The ITL publishes special publications related to security that are freely available for download here: http://csrc.nist.gov/publications/PubsSPs.html.

NOOP – No operation, sometimes listed as NOP. NOOP instructions are often used in a buffer overflow attack. An attacker often writes a large number of NOOP instructions as a NOOP sled into memory, followed with malicious code.

NOS – Network Operating System. Software that runs on a server and enables the server to manage resources on a network.

NTFS – New Technology File System. A file system used in Microsoft operating systems that provides security. NTFS uses the DAC model.

NTLM – New Technology LANMAN. Authentication protocol intended to improve LANMAN. The LANMAN protocol stores passwords using a hash of the password by first dividing the password into two seven-character blocks, and then converting all lower case letters to upper case. This makes LANMAN easy to crack. NTLM stores passwords in LANMAN format for backward compatibility, unless the passwords are greater than 15 characters. NTLMv1 is older and has known vulnerabilities. NTLMv2 is newer and secure.

NTP – Network Time Protocol. Protocol used to synchronize computer times.

OS – Operating system. For example, SELinux is a trusted OS that can help prevent malicious code from executing.

OVAL – Open Vulnerability Assessment Language. International standard proposed for vulnerability assessment scanners to follow.

P2P – Peer-to-peer. P2P applications allow users to share files such as music, video, and data over the Internet. Data leakage occurs when users install P2P software and unintentionally share files. Organizations often block P2P software at the firewall and detect running software with port scans.

PaaS –Platform as a Service. Provides cloud customers with an easy-to-configure operating system, and on-demand computing capabilities. Compare to IaaS and SaaS.

PAP – Password Authentication Protocol. An older authentication protocol where passwords are sent across the network in clear text. Rarely used today.

PAT – Port Address Translation. A form of network address translation.

PBX – Private Branch Exchange. A telephone switch used to telephone calls.

PEAP – Protected Extensible Authentication Protocol. PEAP provides an extra layer of protection for EAP. PEAP-TLS uses TLS to encrypt the authentication process by encapsulating and encrypting the EAP conversation in a Transport Layer Security (TLS) tunnel. Since TLS requires a certificate, PEAP-TLS requires a certification authority (CA) to issue certificates.

PED – Personal Electronic Device. Small devices such as cell telephones, radios, CD players, DVD players, video cameras, and MP3 players.

PGP – Pretty Good Privacy. Commonly used to secure email communications between two private individuals but is also used in companies. It provides confidentiality, integrity, authentication, and non-repudiation. It can digitally sign and encrypt email. It uses both asymmetric and symmetric encryption.

PII – Personally Identifiable Information. Information about individuals that can be used to trace a person's identity, such as a full name, birthdate, biometric data, and identifying numbers such as a social security number (SSN). Organizations have an obligation to protect PII and often identify procedures for handling and retaining PII in data policies.

PIN – Personal identification number. A number known by a user and entered for authentication. PINs are often combined with smart cards to provide two-factor authentication.

PIV – personal identity verification card. A specialized type of smart card used by United States federal agencies. It includes photo identification and provides confidentiality, integrity, authentication, and non-repudiation for the users. It is similar to a CAC.

PKI – Public Key Infrastructure. Group of technologies used to request, create, manage, store, distribute, and revoke digital certificates. Certificates are an important part of asymmetric encryption. Certificates include public keys along with details on the owner of the certificate and on the CA that issued the certificate. Certificate owners share their public key by sharing a copy of their certificate.

POP3 – Post Office Protocol v3. Used to transfer email from mail servers to clients. POP3 uses port 110.

POTS – Plain old telephone service. Voice grade telephone service available.

PPP – Point-to-Point Protocol. Used to create remote access connections.

PPTP – Point-to-Point Tunneling Protocol. Tunneling protocol used with VPNs. PPTP uses TCP port 1723.

PSK – Pre-shared key. A secret shared among different systems. Wireless networks support Personal Mode, where each device uses the same PSK. In contrast, Enterprise Mode uses an 802.1x or RADIUS server for authentication.

PTZ – Pan tilt zoom. Refers to cameras that can pan (move left and right), tilt (move up and down), and zoom to get a closer or a wider view.

RA – Recovery agent. A designated individual who can recover or restore cryptographic keys. In the context of a PKI, a recovery agent can recover private keys to access encrypted data.

RADIUS – Remote Authentication Dial-In User Service. Provides central authentication for remote access clients. RADIUS encrypts the password packets and uses UDP. In contrast, TACACS+ encrypts the entire authentication process and uses TCP.

RAID – Redundant Array of Inexpensive (or Independent) Disks. Multiple disks added together to increase performance or provide protection against faults.

RAID-0 – Disk striping. RAID-0 improves performance but does not provide fault tolerance.

RAID-1 – Disk mirroring. RAID-1 uses two disks and provides fault tolerance.

RAID-5 – Disk striping with parity. RAID-5 uses three or more disks and provides fault tolerance.

RAM – Random Access Memory. Volatile memory within a computer that holds active processes, data, and applications. Data in RAM is lost when the computer is turned off. Inspection of RAM can discover hooked processes from rootkits. Memory forensics analyzes data in RAM.

RAS – Remote Access Service. A server used to provide access to an internal network from an outside location. RAS is also known as Remote Access Server and sometimes referred to as Network Access Service (NAS).

RBAC – Role Based Access Control. An access control model that uses roles to define access and it is often implemented with groups. A user account is placed into a role, inheriting the rights and permissions of the role. Other access control models are MAC and DAC.

RBAC – Rule Based Access Control. An access control model that uses rules to define access. Rule-based access control is based on a set of approved instructions, such as an access control list. Other access control models are MAC and DAC.

RC – Ron's Code or Rivest's Cipher. Symmetric encryption algorithm that includes versions RC2, RC4, RC5, and RC6. RC4 is a secure stream cipher, and RC5 and RC6 are block ciphers.

RFI – Radio frequency interference. Interference from RF sources such as AM or FM transmitters. RFI can be filtered to prevent data interference, and cables can be shielded to protect signals from RFI.

RIPEMD – RACE Integrity Primitives Evaluation Message Digest. A hash function used for integrity. It creates fixed length hashes of 128, 160, 256, or 320 bits.

RPO – Recovery Point Objective. A Recovery Point Objective identifies a point in time where data loss is acceptable. It is related to the RTO and the BIA often includes both RTOs and RPOs.

RSA –An asymmetric algorithm used to encrypt data and digitally sign transmissions. It is named after its creators, Rivest, Shamir, and Adleman, and RSA is also the name of the company they founded together. RSA relies on the mathematical properties of prime numbers when creating public and private keys.

RSTP – Rapid Spanning Tree Protocol. An improvement over STP. STP and RSTP protocols are enabled on most switches and protect against switching loops, such as those caused when two ports of a switch are connected together.

RTO – Recovery Time Objective. An RTO identifies the maximum amount of time it can take to restore a system after an outage. It is related to the RPO and the BIA often includes both RTOs and RPOs.

RTP – Real-time Transport Protocol. A standard used for delivering audio and video over an IP network.

S/MIME – Secure/Multipurpose Internet Mail Extensions. Used to secure email. S/MIME provides confidentiality, integrity, authentication, and non-repudiation. It can digitally sign and encrypt email, including the encryption of email at rest (stored on a drive) and in transit (data sent over the network). It uses RSA, with public and private keys for encryption and decryption and depends on a PKI for certificates.

SaaS – Software as a Service. Applications provided over the Internet. Webmail is an example of a cloud-based technology. Compare to IaaS and PaaS.

SCAP – Security Content Automation Protocol. A method with automated vulnerability management, measurement, and policy compliance evaluation tools

SCP – Secure copy. Based on SSH, SCP allows users to copy encrypted files over a network. SCP uses port 22.

SCSI – Small Computer System Interface. Set of standards used to connect peripherals to computers. Commonly used for SCSI hard disks and/or tape drives.

SDLC – Software Development Life Cycle. A software development process. Many different models area available.

SDLM – Software Development Life Cycle Methodology. The practice of using a SDLC when developing applications.

SELinux – Security-Enhanced Linux. A trusted operating system platform that prevents malicious or suspicious code from executing on both Linux and UNIX systems. It is one of the few operating systems that use the MAC model.

SFTP – Secure FTP. An extension of Secure Shell (SSH) using SSH to transmit the files in an encrypted format. SFTP transmits data using port 22.

SHA – Secure Hash Algorithm. A hashing function used to provide integrity. SHA1 uses 160 bits, and SHA-256 uses 256 bits. Hashing algorithms always provide a fixed size bit-string regardless of the size of the hashed data. By comparing the hashes at two different times, you can verify integrity of the data.

SHTTP – Secure Hypertext Transfer Protocol. An alternative to HTTPS. Infrequently used.

SID – Security identifier. Unique set of numbers and letters used to identify each user and each group in Microsoft environments.

SIM – Subscriber Identity Module. A small smart card that contains programming and information for small devices such as cell phones.

SIRT – Security Incident Response Team. A group of experts that respond to security incidents. Also known as CERT, CERT, or IRT.

SLA – Service level agreement. An agreement between a company and a vendor that stipulates performance expectations, such as minimum uptime and maximum downtime levels.

SLE – Single loss expectancy. Used to measure risk with annualized loss expectancy (ALE) and annualized rate of occurrence (ARO). The SLE identifies the expected dollar amount for a single event resulting in a loss. The calculation is SLE * ARO = ALE.

SMTP – Simple Mail Transfer Protocol. Used to transfer email between clients and servers and between email servers and other email servers. SMTP uses port 25.

SNMP – Simple Network Management Protocol. Used to manage network devices such as routers or switches. SNMP agents report information via notifications known as SNMP traps, or SNMP device traps.

SONET – Synchronous Optical Network Technologies. A multiplexing protocol used to transfer data over optical fiber.

SPIM – Spam over Internet Messaging. A form of spam using instant messaging that targets instant messaging users

SPOF – Single point of failure. An SPOF is any component whose failure results in the failure of an entire system. Elements such as RAID, failover clustering, UPS, and generators remove many single points of failure.

SQL – Structured query language. Used by SQL-based databases, such as Microsoft's SQL Server. Web sites integrated with a SQL database are subject to SQL injection attacks. Input validation with forms and stored procedures help prevent SQL injection attacks. Microsoft's SQL Server uses port 1433 by default.

SSH – Secure Shell. SSH encrypts a wide variety of traffic such as Secure File Transfer Protocol (SFTP), Telnet, and Secure Copy (SCP). SSH uses port 22.

SSID – Service Set Identifier. Identifies the name of a wireless network. Disabling SSID broadcast can hide the network from casual users but an attacker can easily discover it with a wireless sniffer. It's recommended to change the SSID from the default name.

SSL – Secure Sockets Layer. Used to encrypt traffic on the wire. SSL is used with HTTPS to encrypt HTTP traffic on the Internet using both symmetric and asymmetric encryption algorithms. SSL uses port 443 when encrypting HTTPS traffic.

SSO – Single sign-on. Authentication method where users can access multiple resources on a network using a single account. SSO can provide central authentication against a federated database for different operating systems.

SSTP – Secure Socket Tunneling Protocol. A tunneling protocol that encrypts VPN traffic using SSL over port 443.

STP – Spanning Tree Protocol. Protocol enabled on most switches that protects against switching loops. A switching loop can be caused if two ports of a switch are connected together, such as those caused when two ports of a switch are connected together.

STP – Shielded twisted pair. Cable type used in networks that includes shielding to prevent interference from EMI and RFI. It can also prevent data from emanating outside the cable.

SYN - Synchronize. The first packet in a TCP handshake. In a SYN Flood attack, attackers send this packet, but don't complete the handshake after receiving the SYN/ACK packet. A flood guard is a logical control that protects against SYN Flood attacks.

TACACS – Terminal Access Controller Access-Control System. An older remote authentication protocol that was commonly used in UNIX networks. TACACS+ is more commonly used.

TACACS+ – Terminal Access Controller Access-Control System+. Provides central authentication for remote access clients and used as an alternative to RADIUS. TACACS+ uses TCP port 49, compared with TACACS which uses UDP port 49. It encrypts the entire authentication process, compared with RADIUS, which only encrypts the password. It uses multiple challenges and responses.

TCO – Total cost of ownership. A factor considered when purchasing new products and services. TCO attempts to identify the cost of a product or service over its lifetime.

TCP – Transmission Control Protocol. Provides guaranteed delivery of IP traffic using a three-way handshake.

TCP/IP – Transmission Control Protocol / Internet Protocol. Represents the full suite of protocols.

TFTP – Trivial File Transfer Protocol. Used to transfer small amounts of data with UDP port 69. In contrast, FTP is used to transfer larger files using TCP ports 20 and 21.

TKIP – Temporal Key Integrity Protocol. Wireless security protocol introduced to address the problems with WEP. TKIP was used with WPA but many implementations of WPA now support CCMP.

TLS – Transport Layer Security. Used to encrypt traffic on the wire. TLS is the replacement for SSL and like SSL, it uses certificates issued by CAs. PEAP-TLS uses TLS to encrypt the authentication process and PEAP-TLS requires a CA to issue certificates.

TPM – Trusted platform module. This is a hardware chip on the motherboard included on many newer laptops include a TPM. A TPM includes a unique RSA asymmetric key, and it can generate and store other keys used for encryption, decryption, and authentication. TPM provides full disk encryption.

UAT – User Acceptance Testing. One of the last phases of testing an application before its release.

UDP – User Datagram Protocol. Used instead of TCP when guaranteed delivery of each packet is not necessary. UDP uses a best-effort delivery mechanism.

UPS – Uninterruptible power supply. A battery backup system that provides fault tolerance for power and can protect against power fluctuations. UPS provide short-term power giving the system enough time to shut down smoothly, or to transfer to generator power. Generators provide long-term power in extended outages.

URL – Universal Resource Locator. Address used to access web resources, such as http://www.sec-plus.com. Pop-up blockers can include URLs of sites where pop-ups are allowed.

USB – Universal Serial Bus. A serial connection used to connect peripherals such as printers, flash drives, and external hard disk drives. Data on USB drives can be protected against loss of confidentiality with encryption. They combine high volume and transfer speeds with ease of concealment and often result in data leakage.

UTP – Unshielded twisted pair. Cable type used in networks that do not have any concerns over EMI, RFI, or cross talk. If these are a concern, STP is used.

VLAN – Virtual local area network. A VLAN can logically group several different computers together, or logically separate computers, without regard to their physical location. It is possible to create multiple VLANs with a single switch.

VM – Virtual machine. A virtual system hosted on a physical system. A physical server can host multiple VMs as servers. Virtualization can reduce the footprint of an organization's server room or datacenter, and helps eliminate wasted resources. It also helps reduce the amount of physical equipment, reducing overall physical security requirements. A VM escape is an attack that allows an attacker to access the host system from within the virtual system.

VoIP – Voice over IP. A group of technologies used to transmit voice over IP networks. Vishing is a form of phishing that sometimes uses VoIP.

VPN – Virtual private network. Provides access to a private network over a public network such as the Internet. VPN concentrators provide VPN access to large groups of users.

VTC – Video Teleconferencing. A group of interactive telecommunication technologies that allow people in two or more locations to interact with two-way video and audio transmissions.

WAF – Web application firewall. A firewall specifically designed to protect a web application, such as a web server. A WAF inspects the contents of traffic to a web server, can detect malicious content, and block it.

WAP – Wireless access point, sometimes just called an access point (AP). Increasing the power level of a WAP increases the wireless coverage of the WAP. Decreasing the power levels, decreases the coverage. Coverage can also be manipulated by moving or positioning the wireless antenna.

WEP – Wired Equivalent Privacy. Original wireless security protocol. Had significant security flaws and was replaced with WPA, and ultimately WPA2. WEP used RC4 incorrectly making it susceptible to IV attacks.

WIDS –Wireless Intrusion Detection System. An IDS used for wireless networks.

WIPS – Wireless Intrusion Prevention System. An IPS used for wireless networks.

WLAN – Wireless local area network. Network connected wirelessly.

WPA – Wi-Fi Protected Access. Replaced WEP as a wireless security protocol without replacing hardware. Superseded by WPA2.

WPA2 – Wi-Fi Protected Access version 2. Newer security protocol used to protect wireless transmissions. It supports CCMP for encryption, which is based on AES and stronger than TKIP which was originally released with WPA. In Enterprise Mode, it can use RADIUS to support 802.1x authentication. In personal mode, it uses a preshared key (PSK).

WTLS – Wireless Transport Layer Security. Used to encrypt traffic for smaller wireless devices.

XML – Extensible markup language. Used by many databases for inputting or exporting data. XML uses formatting rules to describe the data.

XTACACS – Extended Terminal Access Controller Access-Control System. An improvement over TACACS developed by Cisco Systems and proprietary to Cisco systems. TACACS+ is more commonly used.

XSRF – Cross-site request forgery. An attack that causes users to perform actions on web sites without their knowledge. In some cases, attackers use header manipulation to steal cookies and harvest passwords.

XSS – Cross-site scripting. It scripting allows an attacker to redirect users to malicious web sites and steal cookies. Email can include an embedded HTML image object or a JavaScript image tag as part of a malicious cross-site scripting attack. Web sites prevent cross-site scripting attacks with input validation to detect and block input that include HTML and JavaScript tags. Many sites prevent the use of < and > characters to block cross-site scripting.

Made in the USA
Lexington, KY
27 December 2012